# Hoop Snakes, Hide Behinds and Side-Hill Winders

## Tall Tales from the Adirondacks

By
**Joseph Bruchac**

Illustrated by
**Tom Trujillo**

T0204791

Copyright ©1991 by Joseph Bruchac

"Bill Greenfield and the Championship Wrestler" and "Bill Greenfield and the Mosqui-toes" first appeared in *Cricket Magazine*. "Grampa Jesse and the Used Nails" and "Grampa Jesse and the Patented Corn Planter" first appeared in *Adirondack Life Magazine*.

Cover design by Tom Trujillo
Illustrations by Tom Trujillo

Printed in the U.S.A.

**Library of Congress Cataloging-in-Publication Data**

Bruchac, Joseph, 1942-
    Hoop snakes, hide behinds, and side-hill winders: tall tales from
the Adirondacks/ as told by Joseph Bruchac: illustrated by Tom
Trujillo.
    p. cm.
    ISBN 0-89594-504-5 (cloth) -- ISBN 0-89594-506-1 (pbk.)
    1. Tall tales--New York (state) -- Adirondack Mountain Region.
I. Title.
GR110 . N7B78   1991
398 . 2' 09747 ' 5--dc20                                             91-10361
                                                             CIP

# Hoop Snakes, Hide Behinds and Side-Hill Winders

ALSO BY JOSEPH BRUCHAC

**Return of the Sun**
*Native American Tales from the Northeast Woodlands*

**Iroquois Stories**
*Heroes and Heroines, Monsters and Magic*

**The Wind Eagle**
*And Other Abenaki Stories*

**Keepers of the Earth**
*Native American Stories and Environmental Activities
for Children*

**Survival This Way**
*Interviews with American Indian Poets*

**The Faithful Hunter**
*A Book of Folk Stories*

# CONTENTS

# PART ONE

# BILL GREENFIELD

# Introducing Bill Greenfield

T all tales are still very much a part of the lore of the Adirondacks. Many an Adirondack woodsman, whether it be old Mart Moody of Tupper Lake (who died at the age of 95 in 1912) or a contemporary figure such as Bill Smith of Colton (reknowned for both his pack baskets and his yarns), has outdone Paul Bunyan with his fantastic exploits. One of my favorite characters is a folk hero of the southern Adirondacks named Bill Greenfield. Immortalized in Harold W. Thompson's landmark volume of New York State folklore, *Body, Boots and Britches*, Bill Greenfield was a real person. Born in 1833 in Edinburgh, a little hamlet on the east side of the West Branch of the Sacandaga, he and his father, Abner, were famous for their ability to stretch the truth till it twanged like a banjo string. Just about every little town up there where Saratoga, Fulton, and Hamilton counties come together has claimed Bill and his father as residents at one time or another. Some said that a good many of Bill's stories originated with his father, but by the time of his death in 1903, most of the tall tales in the Greenfield Cycle were attributed to Bill. Growing up in the town of Greenfield Center, just a bit south of Bill's stomping grounds, it is hard for me to say when it was that I first started hearing Bill Greenfield stories. I know

3

that one of my neighbors, Lawrence Older—himself a widely known storyteller and musician—passed on to me some of the Bill Greenfield stories I know. They say Bill is buried in the Clarksville Cemetery, not too far from the town of Edinburgh where he was born. It seems to me, though, as if the real truth may be that Bill is still walking around in those woods that he loved and lied about, for his stories seem even more alive to me today than they did when I first heard them three or more decades ago.

Some people are famous for the deeds they do and some are famous for the stories they tell. Bill Greenfield was famous for both, though it's been said that Bill did tend to stretch things a bit. Now I wouldn't say Bill was what you'd call a liar. A lie is meant to deceive someone and Old Bill Greenfield was no deceiver. He just told what folks up here in the mountains call tall tales, stories that make you listen hard and think even harder, sometimes even laugh a little. Those kinds of stories.

A tall tale, you see, is like the seed of a tree. Once you plant it and it gets rooted firm, it just keeps on growing. It can live on long after the one who planted it is gone. And the stories about Bill Greenfield, those stories he told and the stories told about him are like the tall pines you still see on some of the Adirondack ridgetops, big and blowing in the wind.

Bill Greenfield, they say, was quite a man. He was a champion wrestler, a crack shot, a great hunter, a wonderful logger, and a man with quick wits. Even the devil couldn't get the better of Old Bill. Just listen to these stories and you'll see.

# BILL GREENFIELD'S BREAKFAST

**N**ow as anyone who has worked in the woods can tell you, there's no meal in a day more important to a logger than his breakfast. A man has to be fully fueled in order to tromp off into the big woods for a good eight hours of work before sitting down to a dinner sack for his mid-day meal. And, as the greatest logger of his time, Bill Greenfield always had to have the biggest and the best breakfast.

Bill always prided himself on having a cook who knew his business, a cook who was proud of his work. By the time the crew piled out of their bunks to sit down at the table, Bill's cook would have already been up thirty-six hours before dawn, just to make that morning feed. A typical morning meal would consist of about ten pounds of salt pork, three pecks of potatoes, six dozen eggs, three dozen flapjacks, and twelve pies. And that was just for one small to average size logger.

A logger would also glug down a good five gallons of strong coffee, just enough to get his eyes open, so to speak. Strong coffee in the Adirondacks, by the way, means something more than strong coffee down in the flatlands. Down there, coffee is strong when you stick a spoon in it and the spoon stands up. In the Adirondacks, coffee is strong when you put a spoon in it and the

*Those were the lightest and finest flapjacks ever enjoyed by man or beast.*

spoon dissolves. When they first introduced motorized vehicles into the woods they were using some of that Adirondack coffee for a time in place of battery acid, but they had to give up on it when it started eating the bottom out of the batteries.

Bill's cook always prided himself on making the lightest flapjacks in creation. They was so light that a hummingbird's tongue would have weighed less than a stack of 'em piled two foot high. But, as everyone knows, no matter how good things are, some folks will always complain. Sure enough, one morning, some of the men went jawing on about how the pancakes were overly heavy that day. That made the cook mad and he resolved that the next morning he would make flapjacks that was so feathery no man would ever complain about their not being light enough.

He was up for thirty-seven hours that night, getting ready for breakfast and mixing and remixing his pancake mix, adding more baking powder to the fixin's to make them flapjacks perfect. Next morning, when the men came in for breakfast, they didn't see any pancakes. One of the men took a peek across the dog run between the kitchen and the dining hall and let out a howl. "Jeohosophat!" he yelled. " Look out to the cookshack." Well, the men looked and what did they see but one perfect pancake after another floating out of the window of the cookhouse and up into the air. Every time the cook finished a pancake and put it on the tray, that pancake, which was lighter than air, would just waft up into the breeze and drift up towards the clouds. They never would have gotten to taste any of those pancakes if Bill Greenfield hadn't grabbed his shotgun and started shooting them out of the air. He had to use up ten boxes of shells, but the men said it was worth it for, after they got done picking out the buckshot, those were the lightest and finest flapjacks ever enjoyed by man or beast.

Now after that particular morning, the cook never made flapjacks quite that light again, but he made them so good that no one could ever get enough. One morning, in fact, by the time Bill reached the table, all the flapjacks was completely gone.

"I vow," Bill said, "that from now in there are goin' to be enough flapjacks to go around." Then Bill took to studyin' the situation. He studied and he studied and when he was done studyin' he figured he had figured out the problem. The problem was that there just wasn't a big enough griddle to make up a sufficiency of pancakes.

So Bill went down to the iron works in Albany and had them make up a special griddle to his specifications. It took as much iron as would have gone into 2,327 and one half plows, but when they was done, they had a griddle that looked just right. It wouldn't fit on a freight car to ship it up to the mountains, but Bill was prepared for that. He hitched up his big blue ox named Babe (a name which a young fella by the name of Bunyan would later give to his own blue ox which was, truth be told, just a mite smaller and weaker than Bill's Babe) and headed down for the city. When he got there, he had them turn that griddle on its side, drill a hole in the center—which he could fill in later—and stick in a hub. Then he hitched up Babe and drew that griddle right up into the mountains to his camp just south of Tupper Lake.

Whilst he was fetching that griddle, Bill had his crew working to make a place for that griddle. They cleared twelve acres of woods and leveled the ground and when Bill got there, he unhitched the ox from one side of the hub and had Babe give it one more pull in just such a way that the griddle started spinning. It spun so fast that it dug the ground right out to a depth of a good forty feet and when it flopped down over that hole, neat as can be, all that the loggers had to do was dig tunnels in from the sides so they could pile the wood underneath to heat the grill. They stacked a hundred and forty one cords of wood there and then they started it burning. That grill heated up as nice as can be. Then four dozen loggers tied fatty slabs of bacon to their feet and skated across that griddle to grease it up good.

Bill's cook and his helpers had made up the flapjack mix inside of an old water tower that Bill had set up near the griddle. Chicken wire was strung over the top of that grill, just high enough so the cook and his helpers wouldn't burn themselves whilst they poured on that flapjack mix. There was no way they could flip those big flapjacks, so they just put enough popcorn in so as those pancakes would turn themselves when they got hot enough. Bill had made up some harpoons with good strong rope fastened to them and whenever a flapjack looked to be done they would harpoon it and drag it off the grill.

Well, by the time they were done, they had enough pancakes to satisfy everyone, even Bill. To this day, folks in the Adirondacks talk about that big griddle of Bill's and for years people would make pilgrimages to see it. But when the big war came and the country was short of iron, Bill's patriotic descendents donated that griddle to the war effort and it was used to make a dozen Sherman tanks. The hole where that griddle was filled in with rain over the years and folks today call it Round Lake.

# Bill Greenfield
## and the
# Cold Winter

One of the reasons folks in the Adirondacks were so hardy back in the old days may have been that they had to be tough to survive. Things weren't as easy for folks then as they are now. When it got cold, they couldn't just reach over and turn up the thermostat. They had to tromp out to the wood box and bring in another armful of logs and stoke up the fire. Anyone who's ever woken up in a camp in the woods early in the morning with the stove burned out and their feet half froze knows that keeping a fire going is a serious business. Now Adirondack winters still can be cold. I'll grant you that. I can think of one winter a few years back when the mercury went down so far we had to dig our thermometers three feet out of the ground in the spring. Back in Bill Greenfield's day, though, all the winters were cold. And the one winter when this story took place, it may have been the winter of 1873, just about beat them all.

Bill and his father, Abner were living then in the town of Day, a part of the southern Adirondacks that still gets pretty chilly when the nights grow longer than an Irishman's dream. But the Greenfields were never ones to let a little weather get in their way, though it did lead some folks to say that the Greenfields were the sort who didn't know enough to pull their

*Every time one of those matches would flare up,
though, the flame would freeze solid.*

heads in when they shut the windows.

It was so cold that winter the smoke wouldn't go up the chimney in Abner's house until he rigged up a paddle in the chimney. He put a hinge on one side and then tied a rope to the other and ran it around a pulley he fastened up inside the chimney. Then all he had to do was just keep pulling on the rope to force the smoke up the chimney. After he'd been doing that for a while, though, there was a knock on his door. It was one of the neighbors come to tell Abner that all that smoke in his chimney was freezing just as soon it it hit the air. There was a solid column of frozen smoke eighty-eight feet high and the neighbor was afraid it might fall over and crush someone.

One January day in that same winter, even though it was one of the coldest days they had yet seen, Bill and Abner decided to go out hunting. Now the sun was shining and it didn't seem all that cold at first when they set out, though you did have to pound the air with your fist if you wanted to take a deep breath. But they'd only been walking a short while when one of those cold northern winds, the sort the Indians call "The Great Bear," swept down. The temperature dropped faster than a stone plunked into a stream. Abner and Bill, being as stubborn as burrs on a mitten, weren't about to turn back, though. They figured they'd have skip for supper if they didn't keep on hunting, especially after having told Mrs. Greenfield to put the kettle on the boil for whatever they were going to bag. So they just buttoned up their coats and kept on walking. The rest of the natural world around them, though, was a sight more affected than that. They didn't notice it at first till they got into a piece of woods thick with game. Abner saw a rabbit and was about to take a shot at it when Bill noticed something.

"Hold on!" he said, "What is that there?"

Abner held off his shot and took a look and saw what Bill was pointing at. It was so strange he wasn't quite sure he could believe his eyes.

"Let's get a mite closer," he said to Bill.

So the two of them started to creep up so they wouldn't spook the rabbit. When they got up on it, though, they saw they had no need to be so cautious. That rabbit wasn't about to be spooked. It was frozen solid where it sat and stuck to the ground just as tight as bark to a beech tree. That wasn't what was so strange, though. The strange thing Bill had been pointing at was next to the rabbit. There, frozen solid in mid-leap, was a fox. It was just hanging in the cold air about three feet over that poor rabbit's head.

Bill and Abner decided it just wouldn't of been fair to shoot any animal that was so defenseless, so they just went off and left the rabbit and the fox there. But before they left, Bill who was kind of soft-hearted noticed there was a look of mortal terror frozen into that poor rabbit's eyes. It had seen the fox just about to pounce on it before the cold stopped them both in their tracks. So Bill, thinking ahead to when the spring thaw would come, just moved the fox a little off to the side so that when it unfroze and came down it would miss that rabbit.

Bill and Abner continued on and they saw that day had to have been the coldest one they'd ever known. All around them in that forest everything was frozen still. Even the limbs of the trees were lined with little frozen birds singing little frozen songs. That was when they decided maybe it was too cold after all for hunting. Not only that, Bill's feet were starting to feel a mite cold and they thought they ought to make a fire. The wind was blowing by now and every time they'd try to get some sticks together that wind would pick them up and blow them right out of the county. They decided they'd better take shelter in a nearby cave to warm up. Bill had some of those new safety matches and he started striking them to start a fire. Every time one of those matches would flare up, though, the flame would freeze solid. Now Bill was one who always saved things, even after other folks would have thrown them away and he had in his pocket an empty metal tobacco can. So he pulled that can out and every time one of those matches would light and freeze solid he'd just break off the flame and drop it into the can, ker-plunk. For years after that whenever he needed a light all he had to do was shake out one of those frozen flames and let it thaw. Abner got impatient when Bill couldn't get the fire going and he started to cuss. But it was so cold that the words froze right around his mouth in a thick blue cloud. Bill had to chip away at it and then use the barrel of his gun to pry them off so that his father wouldn't suffocate. That blue cloud of quick-froze cusses fell to the floor of the cave with a big thud! Then Bill went back to work on that fire. He actually managed to get it started and those flames roared up about waist high. But then the cold seeped in and that great big fire froze solid, too.

That was when Bill and Abner decided it was no use and they headed for home. By the time they got there, Bill's feet had gotten so cold that he was suffering from a serious case of frost-bite. His feet were pure white from his toes right on up to his knees. Now Bill, being a good woodsman, knew the best thing to do with frost bite is to rub snow on it or put it in cold water. So he called to his mother to bring him a pan of water real fast. It just so happened that Mrs. Greenfield had that pot of boiling water on the stove. Not knowing what Bill wanted, she lugged it right out to him. Without even hesitating, Bill plunged both his feet right in. That was when he realized just how cold his feet had been. Three inches of ice formed on top of that boiling water before he could count to two! But, even though I wouldn't recommend that treatment to anyone, it did thaw out his frozen feet.

That wasn't the end of it, though. Wouldn't you know that as chance had it the Methodist minister happened to walk past the mouth of that cave just when the spring thaw reached into its depths? Just then, at that exact moment, those cuss words of Abner Greenfield's unfroze and came pouring out. Well, you can guess who was the subject of the Sunday sermon that week!

# Bill Greenfield AND THE Mosquitoes

Up in the mountains, the insects are a lot fiercer than they are in the flatlands. The horseflies are so big that we have to tie the cows down in the fields or they'd carry them off. And we've also got bugs that are so small you wouldn't know they was there until they bit you. There are the punkies which are so tiny that it takes ten men with strong eyesight to see one of them. And then there are the no-see-ums, which no one has ever seen. Some say the worst insects of all are the black flies—which look pretty much like miniature great white sharks with wings—except they are hungrier and much less merciful. I tend to disagree, though. There is nothing more fearsome than a real Adirondack mosquito.

Back in the old days, folks say, the mosquitoes were bigger and fiercer than they are today. Nowadays, around the North Country, it's a rare occasion when you see a mosquito much bigger than a small crow—though there are still a few large ones around. I remember one night when I was camping with my father up on the Cedar River flow I woke up in the night and was just about to step out of the tent. But just as I was about to unzip the flap I thought I heard something and I listened. It was a couple of those big mosquitoes. They were outside our tent hid-

*Up in the mountains, the insects are a lot fiercer than they are in the flatlands.*

ing in the bushes and they were talking to each other.

"Hey," one of them said, "one of them's about to come out. You want to grab him or should I?"

"Let me do it," said the second mosquito. "Should we eat him here or take him down into the swamp."

"Heck no," said the first one. "We take him down there and the big guys will take him away from us!"

Well, as you can imagine, after hearing that, I didn't stir out of that tent till daylight! But mosquitoes of that size are pretty rare now, not like back in Bill Greenfield's day.

One day Bill Greenfield was out skinning out an old horse which had just died for the second time. That horse in itself was quite a story. It was at least 30 years old when it passed away and had been known for miles around because of the stories Bill told about it and because it was so good at drawing a load. When folks would ask Bill why that horse was so strong he'd tell them this story.

Bill had gotten that horse from a local trader known for making sharp bargains. The price had been so good on that horse that Bill just knew there had to be something wrong with it. But after he'd had it for a few months, he figured maybe he'd just outtraded that trader. That horse was gentle and smart and a good worker. It'd go right into its own stall at the end of the day. And everything went along fine until the day when Bill was drawing a load a fence posts on his sledge. He was about four miles from home when, all of a sudden, WHAM! that horse keeled right over in its tracks. Well, Bill figured he'd finally found out what was wrong with that horse. It had a bad heart and now he was stuck with a dead animal. It made him feel pretty bad, not so much because he was outtraded as because he'd grown fond of that beast. He managed to get it unharnessed and then, rather than making a trip back, decided he would skin it right out there on the spot. So he skinned that horse right out, threw the hide up on top of that load, grabbed hold and dragged that sledge back

17

home by himself. Seeing as how it was only four miles and the load didn't weigh more than a ton, he barely worked up a sweat.

When he pulled into his yard, a peddler was just coming down his lane, having sold some kettles to Bill's wife. That peddler saw that horse hide and offered Bill fifty cents for it. That was a good price back then and Bill sold it on the spot. Bill went on in, had his dinner and did his afternoon chores. It was getting towards evening when he remembered—he'd left the barn door open. But as soon as he reached that door, he started to hear a strange noise from the back of the barn. It sounded like somebody either rattling something or tapping out a rhythm. Bill listened close and realized the noise was coming from the direction of his horse's stall. Well, he walked back to take a look, not sure what he'd see, and there, big as life, was his horse. It had only fainted. Soon as it regained consciousness it had walked all the way home and gone right to its stall. But without its skin it was just about froze to death and what Bill had heard were its knees knocking together and its teeth chattering. Bill thought about chasing after that peddler, but it would've been no use—the man was long gone. What was he going to do? His horse was about to freeze to death. Then Bill remembered he had a green moosehide hanging on the fence out back. He went and got it and draped it over his horse's back. That horse seemed real grateful and it warmed up right away. Next day, when Bill went out to the barn, he found that hide had grown right into place and that horse was as good as new. The only difference was that it was twice as strong as any other horse he'd ever seen and it would no longer eat hay or oats. All it wanted in the winter time were twigs and in the summer it would go down to the pond and browse on the water lilies.

Well, it was that horse which had finally died for good and now Bill was going to bury it—rather than try to skin it for a second time which, even after death, didn't seem the fair thing to do. That horse had passed away in the far field, right at the edge of

Bill's sugar bush of maple trees. Bill was a little sloppy about cleaning things up and, even though it was a good three months since the end of the sap run, his big pan they used to cook down the syrup was still there, leaning against a tree.

Bill hadn't gotten too far in digging a hole to bury that horse when he heard a sound that made his blood run cold. If you were to hear that sound today you'd think it was a squadron of B-52s going overhead, but back then a sound like that could mean only one thing. It was a swarm of Adirondack mosquitoes and they were heading his way. Bill looked around. There was not a building within a mile and he didn't have a weapon with him. Those mosquitoes would catch the scent of that dead horse any moment and Bill knew he'd be a goner. He didn't have a weapon on hand to defend himself and he knew it'd do no good to try to hide behind a tree from a flock of mosquitoes. They were so close now he could see their wings knocking the top branches off the trees. He looked around in desperation and then he saw it. That sap pan was right at hand. Bill grabbed it, jumped into the hole, put the sap pan over the top and held his breath.

Sure enough, those mosquitoes came swarming down and the next thing he heard was the most awful slurping and crunching you could imagine as they ate that whole horse, hide, meat, hoof, and bone. Then things got real quiet and Bill thought for a minute they might have gone away. But then a tapping noise started and Bill knew what it was. Those mosquitoes had caught his scent and they were drilling their way right through the metal pan! Before long one of their noses popped through right next to him, but Bill took a stone up off the ground and clinched it right over. Then another one poked through and Bill bent that one, too. Another one and another one and another one and Bill was pounding away like a blacksmith at his anvil, bending over those mosquitoes' beaks. Soon every one of those mosquitoes had drilled their way through the pan and had their noses bent over and stuck! As you might expect, that made every one of those mosquitoes, who even in the best of times have a disposition like a crosscut saw, get *real* angry. They started buzzing their wings to beat all get out. They buzzed so hard they actually lifted that sap pan right straight up in the air. The next thing Bill knew, the old sap pan and all those mosquitoes were disappearing off towards the northeast. Bill Greenfield always said they must have gone on until they got over Lake Champlain and then gotten so tired that they let the weight pull them in and they sank and drowned. "And if you don't believe that's what happened," he'd say, "then how come you don't see no mosquitoes that big around here today?"

And, as the monkey said when he backed into the fan, I guess that is the end of my tale.

# BILL GREENFIELD
# AND THE
# CHAMPION WRESTLER

N ow Bill Greenfield was what you would call a powerful man. They say he was the best wrestler ever seen in Saratoga County and it was because he was so incredibly strong. What kept him in such good shape, he'd tell people, was just doing the everyday work around his farm. Take plowing, for example.

This was back in the days before tractors. To plow your field you'd hitch up the old iron plow behind your horse or your ox and then hold onto the reins and the handles of the plow (just like holding onto the handlebars of a bicycle) to guide it. Bill used an ox for his plowing, but that ox was too slow for Bill. To begin with, Bill got impatient about how long the ox took to come out of its stall in the morning so he just started picking it up and carrying it out to the field to make things go faster. But after the ox was yoked to the plow, it moved even slower yet and Bill would push on the plow to hurry it up. He'd push so hard the ox would have to trot to keep from being run over by the plow. One day Bill just got so fed up with holding back for that ox that he unyoked it and started plowing without it.

Word eventually got out around the state that Bill Greenfield was quite a wrestler and that no man had ever been

*Bill Greenfield smiled and lifted up his arm to point.*
*"Right down that way," he said.*

able to throw him. There was a famous wrestler who lived in Syracuse and he came looking for Bill to challenge him to a match. He lost his way trying to find Bill's home and began looking for someone to give him directions. As chance would have it, the first person he saw was a man plowing his fields. That wrestler leaned against the fence with his mouth open marvelling at the way that man was doing it, plowing without a horse or an ox and just pushing that plow through the rocky soil like a knife through butter. Finally Bill Greenfield took notice of the man and plowed his way over to the fence.

"Can I help ye, stranger?" Bill said.

"Well," said the Syracuse wrestler, taking a deep breath, "I'm a champion wrestler. I've heard there's a man around here named Bill Greenfield who's pretty strong and I thought I might challenge him to a match." The wrestler looked at the heavy iron plow. "But I can see you're a strong man yourself. You must for sure be stronger than him."

Bill Greenfield shook his head. "Nossir," he said, "I'm not stronger than Bill Greenfield. In fact, I can't see any way I could ever beat him in anything."

"Well," said the Syracuse wrestler, "then I guess it's Bill Greenfield I should be looking for. Can you tell me which way his house is."

Bill Greenfield smiled and lifted up his arm to point. "Right down that way," he said.

The Syracuse wrestler looked hard at Bill, for the arm he was pointing with still held onto that heavy plow. Bill was holding it right out at arm's length to point with it. "Thank ye kindly," the Syracuse wrestler said. Then he turned around and walked back the way he came.

# BILL GREENFIELD, THE CRACK SHOT

N ow most people up on the mountain in those days could handle a gun pretty well. You grew up hunting to keep food in the pot and almost any man or boy worth his salt in the woods could bark a squirrel. That meant shooting not at the squirrel itself, which had little enough meat to spoil by hitting it, but to aim so close to the squirrel that the shock of the bullet exploding the bark underneath it would make that animal die of a heart attack. But Bill Greenfield was so good that the squirrels got to know him and all he'd have to do was point his gun at a squirrel and it would just fall out of the tree in expectation of its inevitable end. Bill learned how to shoot from his father, Abner, who was known to be able to knock a fly out of the air in midflight. Bill did him one better by managing to do the same thing without killing the fly, only stunning it enough to knock it unconscious for a little while. It got to the point where saying that the Greenfields were good shots was like saying the sun came up in the east.

Bill and his father even invented a little game when they were living up near Stony Creek that would have made normal human beings just a bit nervous. They'd load up, stand back to back, each walk twenty paces, then turn and fire. Their aims were

*"Why, I wouldn't lie for one pigeon."*

so good and they had it timed so well that the bullets would strike in mid-air and fall to the ground between them. Then, just to see who got his shot off first, they'd measure the distance from the place those bullets fell. One time, though, there was almost a tragedy, for Bill's gun misfired. But Abner's reflexes were so fast that he sensed it immediately and aimed so that his bullet went right down the barrel of Bill's gun without hurting him.

Bill once told the story about the time when he was hunting up around the Beecher's Vly and he saw ninety-nine pigeons all sitting in a line in the limb of a chestnut tree. After watching them for a while he decided he'd see if he could get a shot in. Then he discovered that a hole had torn in his ammunition pouch. He'd lost all his bullets. That didn't stop him for long, though. He opened up his jackknife and loaded it into the gun, took careful aim and fired. The knife split the limb open and when it snapped back it caught every one of those pigeons by the toes.

When Bill first told that story one of the listeners said, "Ninety-nine pigeons?  Why didn't you just make it an even hundred and have done with it?"

Bill Greenfield looked at him in amazement and said, "Why, I wouldn't lie for one pigeon."

There were times, though, when Bill had to admit that even he got lucky. He was out hunting near Third Lake just north of Lake Luzerne for deer and had but one bullet left. Suddenly, there right in front of him were two fine bucks. One was off to his left and the other to his right. Right in between them and closer to Bill there was this peaked rock. Bill studied the situation a bit and saw that if he aimed just right he'd be able to split his bullet on that boulder and the two halves could go on and get both of those bucks. But to take that shot he had to back up just a bit. He moved real slow and got himself right into position, even though it meant he had to put one foot right on top of a mossy rock in the lake and the other foot just on the edge of the shore. He fired and the bullet hit the rock, PING, and down went both bucks. But the kick of the gun was enough to knock Bill off balance and he fell, head over teacup, right back into the lake. When he stood up, though, he had a beaver in his right hand, a muskrat in his left and his overalls were so full of trout they popped the button off in front and it flew right out and killed a partridge!

# Bill's Wonderful Dog

Since Bill was such a good shot, it was only natural that he had the best dog in three counties. Once it got onto the scent it never stopped. One day Bill was out in the woods around Batchelorville doing some cutting and he took his dog along. Bill had an ax that was sharper than a horse trader's wits. Back in those days woodsmen prided themselves on how sharp their axes were and often said that they kept their ax keen enough to shave with and shiny enough to check your reflection in to see if the shave was close enough. Bill's ax, though, was so sharp that you could drop a hair on it and it would slice it right in half down the middle. It was so sharp that its shadow passing over a branch would slice right through it. It was so sharp that you could get cut just by thinking about it. That day Bill's mind was on other things and he got a mite careless. He worked for about two hours, cut and stacked and split four cords of wood and decided it was time for him to take a break before he worked up a sweat. He'd brought a sandwich with him and he figured this was a good time to eat. But when he sat down to eat his lunch he chunked his ax into the base of a nearby tree so that one of the edges was facing out.

At this time, I'd like to tell you a little bit about animal

Bill said that dog turned out to be even better than it was before.

tracks. If you ever go into a field after a snow, the first thing you'll probably see is rabbit tracks. Rabbits love to run around in new snow. Now a rabbit's tracks look just like a set of exclamation points. They run so that the front feet come down first and then the hind legs land in front of those front ones. But if you look closely at those tracks, you just might notice something. One set of tracks is slightly in front of the other. That is because animals, like people, favor either their right or their left sides. Where people are right-handed or left-handed, animals are right-footed or left-footed. If you look at those rabbit tracks right, you can tell whether it was a right-footed or a left-footed rabbit. Another thing about rabbits is this. If you've ever hunted rabbits you'll know the way to do it is for your dog to jump the rabbit and start it running. All you have to do is stand right where you were when that rabbit started in running and you'll get a shot because rabbits always run in a big circle when they're being chased and come back to the place they started from. And if they're a right-footed rabbit they'll run to the right and if they're a left-footed rabbit they'll circle to the left.

Well, just as Bill sat down to eat his lunch, he startled a rabbit from a nearby bush and his dog caught the scent right away and started after it. But it wasn't one rabbit, it was two. Not only that, one of those rabbits was a right-footed rabbit and one was a left-footed rabbit. They headed right towards that tree where Bill had chunked in his double-bitted ax. And the right-footed rabbit went to the right and the left-footed rabbit went to the left. The dog tried to follow them both and cut himself right clean in half from one end to the other. Those two halves of that dog went on running for another twenty feet before they flopped onto their sides.

Bill Greenfield was always quick-witted, though, and he knew just what to do. He grabbed hold of both halves of that dog and slapped them together so fast they didn't even bleed. Then he whipped out the needle and thread he always carried just in case he tore his pants out in the woods and sewed the halves back to-gether again. He did it so fast that dog didn't even feel any pain. Bill had been just a bit too fast, though. In his haste to put his dog back together again he put the right half on right-side up and the left half on upside-down! Two of that poor dog's legs were point-ing straight up at the sky and two were pointing down to the ground. When it tried to stand up it flopped over on its side. But that dog of Bill's was smart. It learned how to run on two legs. In the long run, Bill said that dog turned out to be even better than it was before. When one set of legs got tired, it would just flip it-self over and run on the other two.

# BILL
# AND
# THE DEVIL

W hen it comes to yarn-spinning there's many a man who might say they were just about as good as Bill Greenfield, but it would be hard to find one who could make the boast that they got the best of the Prince of Liars himself, Beelzebub. But some say that Bill Greenfield did that very deed.

It seems Bill was out working in his fields when there was a sudden puff of smoke and the smell of brimstone filled the air and there in front of him stood Old Nick.

"Bill Greenfield," the Devil said, "your time has come. I'm taking you with me."

"Now hold on a minute there," Bill said. "I've heard you're a sporting man, Satan. Isn't there some way you could gimme a last chance."

That pleased the Devil, who always likes gambling, since it brings him so many hapless souls. "I'll tell you what," he said, with an evil grin, "I'll give you three chances to think of just one thing I cannot do."

Bill Greenfield sat down and looked around. There was a huge old elm stump there in the middle of his field. Two yoke of oxen hadn't been able to budge that stump and he'd been plowing around it for three years and cussing it every time. "Well," Bill

Then the Devil reached out and picked up the stone and squeezed it into fine powder so fast that water came right out of the rock.

said, "can you pull up that there stump."

The Devil reached out with one hand and plucked up the stump as if it were a daisy and then gave it a nonchalant fling that landed it smack in the middle of the Atlantic Ocean. And a cold wind began to blow.

Bill looked around again. There was a boulder at the end of the field. Even dynamite hadn't been able to move it out of the way. "Old Scratch," Bill said, "Y'think you can squeeze water outa that there stone?"

Then the Devil reached out and picked up the stone and squeezed it into fine powder so fast that water came right out of the rock. The ground began to shake and the smell of fire and brimstone filled the air and the Devil smiled, certain he would soon have Bill's soul.

But then Bill Greenfield grinned. "Satan," he said, "tell me now, can you find a liar anywhere bigger than old Bill Greenfield?"

And right then and there, the Devil sat down and cried. And when he was done he disappeared in a puff of smoke and he never did bother Bill Greenfield again.

# BILL
# THE
# LOGGER

**M**ost folks in our part of the country agree that there was never another logger to match Bill Greenfield. And if anyone doubted that Bill was the best of 'em all, all they had to do was ask Bill himself and he'd set the record straight. Whether it came to bucking a cut off saw, riding a flying drive down river, breaking jams, or just shouldering his turkey down the skid road at the end of the season, there was none who could match him. Bill never was a jumping jack, one of them who rests all week and works on Sunday, he was regular whirlwind in the woods, known to take a double-bitted ax in either hand, start spinning and bring down enough logs in an hour to keep twenty men limbing and two teams hauling for a week.

Good as he was, though, Bill was only human and as likely to make a mistake now and then as the next man. Bill was sure-footed as a squirrel and there was not a jack who could beat him at a game of Riding the Mule—with two husky shanty boys holding the shaft of a cant hook between them while another man proves his surefootedness by balancing on that narrow stalk till he falls off. The last time Bill played that game—before he was banned from it for life in the log camps—the two jacks who was holding that cant dog and had started off smooth-shaven

*Quick as a cat grabbing a rat Bill grabbed hold of his own ankles.*

grew beards down to their waists waiting for Bill to touch the floor. The tale is still told up to Speculator about the one time Bill did slip off a log. It was in mid-stream on the raging Sacandaga River in the midst of a big drive. He went off head first and when he came up his legs were sticking up in the air on one side of a big log and his head and arms were on the other side. Quick as a cat grabbing a rat Bill grabbed hold of his own ankles and held on like death till the drive pulled up in dead water. Two other jacks came out on the logs and tried to yank Bill out.

"Forget about me," Bill said, " I may be stuck but that poor fella whose legs I got a hold on must be drowned by now!"

The length of an average log drive varied depending on the length or toughness of a river and whether or not the foreman wanted to ram the logs down the river on a flying drive or take his time, sending men back to pick the rear, freeing those logs stranded on rocks and banks after the main drive had gone down river. It might take a few days and it might take weeks. And, as one old logger said to me the other day when I asked him how long it would take the whole drive to come down to the mill:

"Well, the last time we drove the Hudson was in 1953 and some of them logs ain't reached Glens Falls yet!"

Without a doubt, though, the longest drive that ever took place in the Big Woods was one that Bill Greenfield set out on. Bill had gotten together a crew of his own and set out to log so deep in the woods that it would take two weeks to find the place when you were looking at a map. Bill had cruised the edge of that area and seen some standing timber there the likes of which few men have ever set eyes upon. Some of those trees were so tall it'd take three men to see to the top.

Just to give you an idea of how tall those trees were, I have to explain a game that some of the shanty boys used to play back then called "runnin' the trunk." What that meant was that a man would get a tree cut to the point when it was starting to fall and just when it was at the right angle, he would jump up on that trunk with his spiked shoes and start running up it. The objective was to reach the top before it hit the ground and then jump off at just the right moment so as to avoid getting hurt. Bill had respect for those real big trees and he wouldn't let his crew cut any of them. As a matter of fact, some of those real big ones may still be back there in those deep woods. But Bill did decide to cull out some of the pretty big ones which was growing too close together, thinning 'em out, so t' speak. The biggest of those trees that he thinned was tall enough for him to figure that if he was to run that trunk he might be able to set a record of some kind. So, as soon as the cut was deep enough, he yelled to the boys, "Pull the saw free!" jumped up onto that trunk and started to run. He ran so fast that sawdust was flying out from under his feet as if they was a buzzsaw. He ran and he ran and that tree was still falling. Minutes passed and then hours as he ran. Fortunately, Bill had guessed that tree was even taller than it looked and he'd brought a lunch along with him which he ate without even breaking stride. It was just turnin' to twilight when the top of that tree reached the earth and Bill jumped free just at the exact right moment! As soon as he looked around, he knew that no one was ever going to equal what he'd done that day because there was the Pacific Ocean in front of him and he'd landed in the state of Oregon.

Waiting for Bill to get back where he'd started from did delay things a bit for Bill's crew, especially since he had to return on a steam ship around Cape Horn, but Bill figured they would make up for lost time quick enough, especially if they just cut the smaller trees. He'd found a good spot to deck the logs up on a stream they'd dammed up, just as soon as the ice was thick enough, and it was a clean flow downhill to the river. That river was one that Bill and his crew had never driven before, but they guessed that it had to be a feeder stream to another river that would come out somewhere in familiar territory and they could drive the rest of the way down to whatever mill was closest. It was a pretty little river and they built their shanty right next to its banks. So, all that winter, they cut and dragged and had a good pile of logs ready to go when that ice went out and the river was ready to drive.

That winter had been one with a lot of snow—no need to send road monkeys out to make an Irish snowstorm along any of the drag roads the teams followed to bring the logs down to the lake—and so when the thaw came, that river was flowing strong. They raised the gates and the drive dumped into that stream and they were off! It was only after they were a good ten miles downstream that Bill remembered he'd left his good jackknife sitting next to the stove in the ram's pasture of the main shanty. But it was too late to go back and there was a log drive to tend to, and before long Bill forgot about that knife.

The river had a good bend to it, but the water was deep and the flow steady and they made better time than on any other drive Bill had ever been on. Not a single jam and almost every log floating straight as an arrow from the front to the rear. Day after day they went on and still there wasn't any sign of the stream emptying into another bigger river. It just stayed about the same width, smooth as glass and quicksilver swift. Finally after about two weeks they floated past an abandoned log camp. That made Bill and his crew take heart. Though Bill could see that shanty wasn't near as well built as theirs had been, it meant that someone else in the past had driven that river and so it had to dump out somewheres near a mill. So they went, on and on and never a sign of another stream. By now they were running low on some supplies; even though they could still get plenty of woods beef, they were running low on flour and tobacco and the men were starting to complain. But they didn't complain too loud, since Bill Greenfield was always known as the head moose cat in the woods and not a man to try to take ahold of. Once again they floated past an abandoned log camp, one that looked to be in even worse shape than the one they'd passed a fortnight before and again Bill figured they must be getting within range of an end to this drive. So they kept on going, week after week, passing even more log camps. Finally, Bill could go no further. Something was bothering him. When they came to still another shanty built near the river he pulled in to shore and walked over to take a look. That log camp was just falling apart and as he came closer he wondered how anyone with a lick of pride could put together a place in such a slipshod fashion. Although, he had to admit, there was something hauntingly familiar about the place and a terrible notion come over him. He walked into the room in the main shanty where the men gathered at night to listen to tales, the place everyone called the Ram's Pasture. There, sure enough, was a rusty old pot-bellied stove. And right on top of it was Bill's own jackknife.

When Bill came out, he was shaking his head. He called the men in off the river and told them what had happened. There was nothing they could do but swallow their pride and find the trail to walk back home, leaving those logs behind them, still floating along the river. Perhaps those logs are still driving themselves down that river—at least that's what some of the old shanty men say when they tell the story of how Bill Greenfield made the Great Round River Drive.

# How Bill's Wife
Taught Him
a Thing or Two

I n most cases, Bill Greenfield's quick wits were always
enough to get him out of any scrape. But there was at
least one time when Bill's wife had to get him out of trouble. It
seems that Bill was down to the store and, as usual, yarning
about the wonderful things he'd done and seen. Most of the lo-
cals were only half-listening, having heard Bill all too many
times before. But then a little boy come up and started to listen
in and Bill could see that boy was just hangin' on his every word.

"Let me tell you, son," Bill said, " about the way it is up on
my farm. I have got some animals there that really beat all. If you
was to come out to my farm and see them you would think that
your visit was the most wonderful thing you ever done. "

By now that little boy was sitting wide-eyed at Bill's feet.
"Tell me about 'em," Mr. Greenfield," he said and that was all that
Bill needed to hear.

"Well," Bill said, "first of all there's my chickens. You've
heard of your Rhode Island Reds and your Plymouth Rocks and
your White Leghorns, I'm sure?"

That little boy nodded. "Yes, I sure have."

"Well," Bill said, "what I have up to my farm is none of
those. I have an entire new kind of chicken that I have bred my-

*I have an entire new kind of chicken that I have bred
myself and I call 'em Greenfield Giants.*

self and I call 'em Greenfield Giants. Those chickens are so big that one drumstick would feed the whole volunteer fire department. And after we've eaten one of them eggs—which, when cooked up right, makes us enough scrambled eggs for a month—we cut the shells in half lengthwise and sell 'em as porcelain bathtubs. Those chickens are so big that when I feed 'em I have to scatter the corn up on the roof of the barn. They're so tall they don't go around scratching in the barnyard like ordinary fowl, they just walk around in the woods eating the acorns off the tops of the oak trees."

"Those sure are *big* chickens," that little boy said.

"Why if you think those chickens are somethin'," Bill Greenfield said, "you ought to see my dog. That dog is the smartest dog that ever walked on four legs. Now most people, they talk about a smart dog, they just mean it can fetch and shake hands and the like. That dog of mine don't bother with such things. That dog can add, subtract, and multiply. It knows the name of all the presidents and it can recite the Preamble to the Constitution in French. We would've sent it off to college if it wasn't for the fact that it would have gotten homesick being away so long. The only thing it can't seem to do is tell a lie and so we decided not to let it run for Congress. Eh-yup, that dog is so smart it can teach school!"

"That's the smartest dog I *ever* heard of," the little boy said.

"Well," Bill said, "you ought to see my horse, then. That horse is the fastest horse that ever lived. Only reason I don't ride it into town too often is that it's so fast that it wears out ten pairs of horseshoes in a week and I can't afford to keep it shod if I ride it too often. It's so fast that if you was to ride it around the mountain you'd meet yourself coming back the other way. That horse is so fast that I can ride it from here to Boston and back in an hour!"

"That must be the *fastest* horse that ever was," the little boy said.

By the time Bill finished talking, that little boy figured that Bill Greenfield was about the greatest man who'd ever lived to have such wonderful animals as that. And when the boy left, Bill sat there for a while by the stove, feeling real proud of himself for having such an admirer.

"Bill," the storekeeper said, "that little fella there believed every word you said. It's just goin' to break his heart if he finds out that you was just lyin' to him."

"Pshaw," Bill Greenfield said, "He ain't a-goin' to find out any such a thing. Why he'll probably forget all about what I told him before the end of the day."

When Bill went home, he pretty much forgot about all those tall tales he'd told that little boy until the weekend rolled around. Bright and early Saturday morning he looked out the window and what do you suppose he saw? There was that little boy just coming down the lane.

"Oh My Lord," said Bill to his wife, who had just finished making a batch of her famous sugar cookies, "here comes that little boy I was yarnin' to down at the store the other day. He's walked all the way out here from town just to see my chickens that are so tall they eat the nuts off the trees, my dog that's so smart it can teach school and my horse that's so fast it can go from here to Boston and back in an hour. It's going to break his heart when I can't show him none of those things. What am I goin' t'do?"

"Bill," Mrs. Greenfield said, "I knew your stories were going to get you into trouble one of these days. You just hide under the bed and I'll see if I can pull the fat out of the fire for you. And maybe I can even teach you a thing or two about storytelling. "

Bill crawled under the bed and got hid just as the little boy knocked. Wiping her hands on her apron, Mrs. Greenfield answered the door.

"Good day, M'am," said the little boy. "I come out here from town to see if Mr. Greenfield could show me those big chickens of his."

"I'm sorry, young man, " Mrs. Greenfield said, "but Bill's not here right now and we have sent those chickens down to my brother's in Charlton. We ran all out of chicken feed and my brother's got a lot of acorns in of his oak trees that they can eat in the meantime."

The little boy looked downcast for a minute, but then he brightened up. "Can I see that dog of Mr. Greenfield's that's so smart it can teach school?" he said. "I'd just love to hear how it can talk French."

"I'm sorry to disappoint you for the second time, young man," said Mrs. Greenfield, "but it seems the school teacher over in Galway took sick this week. That dog's going to be over there for the next ten days or so substitute teaching."

That little boy looked sad, but then he smiled again. "Well," he said, "I guess I can just see that fast horse of his, then."

Mrs. Greenfield shook her head. "I hate to tell you this," she said, "but Bill took that horse. As I said, we run out of feed and so Bill just left to go to Boston and get some more. He said he had another errand to run down to New York City right after that so he probably won't be back for at least three hours. But I'll tell you what I can show you. I've got a cookie jar back here that is dangerously full and I think maybe you can help me with it."

That little boy brightened right up. "I'd be happy to help you, Ma'am," he said.

By the time he left, after helping out by eating an adequate amount of those sugar cookies, for which Mrs. Greenfield was rightfully famous, that little boy thought his visit out to the Greenfield farm was the most wonderful thing he'd ever done. And Bill Greenfield, who had to stay hidden under that bed and didn't even get a single one of those cookies, did indeed learn a lesson that day about storytelling from his wife.

45

# Bill Greenfield
## and the
# Big Old Bear

One fine fall day Bill Greenfield went out grouse hunting. For one reason or another on this particular day, Bill didn't take along his special over and under hound, the one with two legs that pointed up and two that pointed down. But he did take his favorite double-barreled shotgun. Now Bill believed in safety when he was afield, so it was his practice never to load his gun until he reached the spot where he was going to start hunting.

He decided to take a short cut through the thick woods over Forked Hill. Bill's mind was wandering a bit that day or he would have realized that the familiar path had one more rise in it than normal. As it was, he took two steps up onto what he thought was a little hill when that hill shook itself and threw him to the ground. Bill looked up to see, rising on its hind legs above him the biggest bear he had ever seen. It had been sleeping right there in the middle of the path and Bill had disturbed its slumber.

Well now, that big old bear was not happy! It let out a roar so loud that Bill was deaf for three weeks after that. The fact that he'd been deafened didn't make no never mind to Bill at that particular moment. Just then his ears were a lot less important

That bear must have seen other folks with guns before because it lifted that gun right up to its shoulder and pointed it up at Bill like he was about to shoot him out of the tree.

to him than his feet!

Bill took off, his legs a-spinning so fast he wore a groove in the earth three foot wide and ten foot long. It was fortunate for Bill that he moved as quick as he did. That big old bear took a great swipe at him. Its paw missed Bill, but the wind from it took Bill's hat right off his head and blew it all the way into the next county! Bill kept his feet a-moving just as fast as he could. He figured he was leaving that bear far behind—until he noticed that he wasn't making any more forward progress than a slow saunter.

He looked over his shoulder and saw that dang bear sitting about twenty feet back there with a smug look on its face and its claws hooked right into Bill's suspenders. Well, Bill reached down and unsnapped those suspenders quicker than a cat can lick its ear. Those suspenders popped back so fast that bear was knocked back nigh onto a hundred yards as Bill took off like an arrow, holding his pants up with one hand and clutching his empty shotgun with the other.

Bill knew right where he was heading. There was a great elm tree half a mile down that path. Bill hightailed it for the elm with that big bear galloping behind and getting closer with every stride. Bill reached that tree and swarmed up that trunk so quick he wore off all the bark on one side as smooth as if it had been drawshaved. In doing so, though, he had to drop his shotgun. He went up so fast that he climbed forty foot up above the top of the tree before he realized he'd run out of branches and he had to climb down real fast before he began to fall. Then, wrapping both arms around a branch, Bill looked below.

There, at the bottom of the tree, sat the big old bear, looking up at him, sort of wistful. That bear was too heavy to climb a tree and that old elm was too big for it to reach up to get Bill or to knock the tree down. Bill smiled, figuring he was safe and that sooner or later that old bear would get bored and move along.

But then that big old bear picked up Bill's shotgun. That

bear must have seen other folks with guns before because it lifted that gun right up to its shoulder and pointed it up at Bill like he was about to shoot him out of the tree. As Bill later said, that bear was just about the smartest bear he ever did see. That old bear was so smart that it realized there was something wrong, snapped open the gun, peered down the breech and got this disappointed look on its face when it saw it wasn't loaded. Bill sat up there in the tree feeling real thankful that all the shells for that shotgun were still safe in his coat pocket!

Then, Bill said, that big old bear did its first dumb thing. It looked up at Bill and started making motions that took Bill a moment to understand. It was begging Bill to throw some shells down to it!

# How Bill Greenfield
# Moved in with
# the Bears

N ow Bill Greenfield wasn't usually one to run from a bear. That big old bear hadn't really spooked Bill, just startled him so much that Bill didn't have the time to let his feet know that he wasn't really scared. As Bill explained, if he'd just had a moment he could have reasoned with that bear. Bill Greenfield, you see, was one of the few people in the Adirondacks who could speak bear talk. As a matter of fact. Bill was more or less adopted by the bears and this is how it came to be.

Many years ago, when Bill Greenfield was a young man, he was part of a crew that was logging deep in the woods up in Township 19. Bill always enjoyed getting off and working by himself and he'd even built a little shanty of his own a mile or so from the main bunkhouse. All it had in it was a stove and a cot with a big warm bearskin robe so that even when the winds blew cold Bill could wrap up in it and be warm as a flea in a dog's ear. He'd head back to the main camp whenever he was low on food or in need of a little company, of course.

This one particular day, Bill had been working away skinning hemlock logs with a spud. As anyone knows, hemlock floats like a rock unless the bark is off it. But spudding a hemlock is messy, dirty work and there was an overly adequate supply of

*Not only were bears more generous than most humans, they were a dang sight more interesting to talk to.*

mosquitoes that particular sunny day and so Bill kept swatting them while he was skinning off the bark and by the time the day was done he was pretty well gunked up with pitch from the top of his head to the bottom of his feet. He was as sticky and black as a turkey buzzard's neck. He'd worked a lot longer than he'd intended, too, and he was about as wore out as the soles of a twenty-year old pair of boots. He was so tired, in fact, that he didn't bother to wash up or have a bite to eat or even shut the door when he got back to his little shanty. He just collapsed onto that cot, rolled the bearskin robe around him and went fast to sleep. He was so tired that he slept two days straight. Whilst he was asleep, the raccoons crept right in through that open door and stole every bit of Bill's grub.

When Bill woke up, he was as hungry as he didn't know what, but when he went to his little larder he found all the food was gone. His stomach was growling now so loud that it scared the birds out of the trees for half a mile around. Bill was feeling desperate for food and he headed right out for the main camp a mile away, animals taking flight in all directions as the sound of his growling stomach went with him through the woods.

Bill come up over the little rise above the camp and started down the hill towards the cookhouse at a good clip. But as he did so, he saw that things were strange. All the folks in the camp were staring up the hill and as he got closer they started to hightail it in all directions.

"BEAR!" someone was shouting. "BEAR IN THE CAMP."

"GOOD LORD," another person yelled. "THAT'S THE UGLI-EST LOOKING BEAR I EVER SEEN!"

Bill looked behind him, but he was danged if he could see any bear. He turned around and was about to yell back at the others, "What Bear?" when a shotgun blast tore up the ground right in front of him. Bill jumped and the next blast hit a tree right where he'd been standing. Why in tarnation someone was shooting in his direction Bill couldn't begin to guess, but he figured he'd better make himself scarce in the meantime!

He turned around and started to run for it, shot spattering all around him. Folks had gone hog wild! He ran so low to the ground he was right on all fours. He ran up over the ridge and kept on going. He ran right over the top of Porter Mountain and down into the valley on the other side. When he stopped running he had gone a good ten miles as the crow flies.

Bill flopped down, trying to make heads or tails of what had been happening back in camp. He reached up to wipe the sweat off his forehead wondering why he was so hot. After all, he hadn't put his coat on when he left his little shanty. As soon as he saw what was stuck to his arm—and for that matter to the rest of him—he realized that he was wearing something after all! He stood up and took a good look at himself. He'd had so much pitch on him after spudding out those trees, that bear skin robe of his had stuck to him. And right away he figured out just who that ugly bear was that the other loggers had got so het up about. It was him!

Well, Bill tried to peel that skin off him, but by now the pitch had set and it was stuck so tight there was no way short of skinning himself that he could get free. Bill was in a pickle! His one hope was to get some kerosene to dissolve that pitch. But the only kerosene for fifty miles around was back in the camp and there was no way Bill was about to go into camp looking like a bear.

Bill thought a bit and then decided the best thing he could do would be to wait till it was dark and things was quieted down. Then he could sneak in and steal some kerosene. And then, by thunder, when he'd got out of that bear robe, he'd have a bone to pick with the logger who'd made that remark about him being the ugliest bear he'd ever seen!

It was still a while till dark, though, so Bill just curled up to take another nap. He wasn't sure how long he slept, but he woke up real fast when he felt a big tongue licking his face. He opened his eyes to see that tongue was connected to the mouth of a bear that was standing right over him! He looked around and saw three more bears. Bill froze, sure they were about to tear him apart. Instead, though, they come up and all started licking and nuzzling him and making all kinds of noises that Bill took to be sounds of welcome. It was like they were greeting an old friend. Figuring, as the old saying goes, that it is better to lick 'em and to join 'em, Bill started to do the same. Those bears seemed just as happy as clams. Next thing he knew, one of them come up with a comb of honey in its mouth and dropped it right in front of Bill. Bill was about starved and he gobbled that honey right up. That seemed to please those bears and they brought Bill some more to eat. Before long, Bill had to admit to himself that he was feeling right to home. Then those bears started off up the trail and they nudged Bill along with them.

Well, that was the last of human habitation that Bill was to see for the next few seasons. Maybe it was just that Bill had grown used to life in the log camps, but he was to say in later years that living among the bears was a darn sight more civilized than human companionship. Not only were bears more generous than most humans, they were a dang sight more interesting to talk to and you'd sure as blazes never see one bear try to deceive another.

Bill got to like the bears so well he started pointing out the traps that was set for them and helping them avoid human hunters. When the winter come, he hibernated right along with those bears and the next spring and summer he went along berry-picking and fishing in the streams. Bill probably would have been among those bears still if that bear robe hadn't started to wear away. Bill held it together as best he could, trying to keep it fastened onto him with vines and such, but one morning he woke up and found the bears was gone. He stood up and the little tatters of bearskin fell off of him and he knew he was going to have to go back to being a human being again.

Ever after that, Bill Greenfield never would abide anyone even talking about hunting a bear around him. It got so folks would hide their bearskin rugs whenever they saw Bill Greenfield coming because they knew once they turned their backs on him Bill would have that bearskin up around his shoulders and be heading off up into the woods. Whether he would be trying to convince the bears to let him join them again or just to give that skin a decent burial, no one ever knew.

# PART TWO

# GRAMPA JESSE

# Grampa Jesse
## and the
## Used Nails

L ast July, I was doing some fixing around the old house my Grandfather Jesse Bowman built. I was raised in that house and I still live there with my wife and our two sons, so I know all sorts of stories connected with that place. I was about to put in a new window, so I was clearing the space on the outside wall, trying to salvage what I could to use for repairs on other parts of the building. But when I took the newer siding off I came to a layer of old wooden shingles. Shakes is what folks used to call them—handmade each one, split from a log block. As I started prying them off I noticed something strange. Just about every one of them had extra holes in them—as if nails have been driven in and pulled out. I was puzzled for a minute till I remember I was working on the southeast side of the house and I slapped my leg. That was it, all right! Grampa Jesse and those used nails.

Grampa Jesse, you see, was a man who saved things. He kept balls of twine, old newspapers, tin foil, broken furniture. He had rings of keys for doors that had long ago been taken off and for cars that had been traded in or gone to the junk yard thirty years ago. He had a lumber room full of odd pieces of board and the shelves of the three-corner cupboard in the kitchen were lined with empty patent medicine bottles, empty cigar boxes and

*There wasn't but one solitary shingle still stuck to the wall, hanging by a single nail. That was strange enough, but stranger still was the fact that there was a robin flapping around that one shingle.*

tobacco tins. He didn't hold with throwing away nothing that might have of been old and a little bunged up, but still had some use left in it—even if it was just to prop up something that was lacking a leg or otherwise in need of repair. He wore an old beach jacket that was threadbare and had holes in its pockets from his habit of sticking his pipe into it still smoldering after he'd smoked all he cared to smoke just then. He never knocked out the ashes because there might still be some good tobacco left in there he could smoke later. As a result of that, there was many a time as a child when I would have to tell him, "Grampa, you're on fire!" and then watch him pound out a smoking pocket with his palms.

I suppose that's where my habit of saving things comes from, now that I think of it. For example, I still have his old hammer, which had real sentimental value to him. It was easy to understand why, because that hammer once saved him from a bad fall. It seems that one summer evening he was up on the roof working. He never was one afraid of heights, maybe because of the Indian blood in him. He was just as sure-footed as a squirrel in a beech tree. That evening, though, he put his hammer down on the roof when he was finished and stepped back onto his ladder to take a look at what he'd done. As ill chance would have it, the top rung of that old ladder was so worn out that it broke right through and he went off that roof head over teakettle! He would've broken something for sure if it wasn't for the fact that halfway down to the ground he remembered he'd left his hammer up on the roof and he had to go back up to get it. So you can see why he prized that hammer. It had been in our family so long that he was sure it was a real antique and probably worth some money, but he wouldn't take any amount of cash for that hammer. Why, it had been in our family for so long that its handle had been changed four times and its head. And I've changed the handle and the head once myself in the thirty years I've had it, so there's no way I'd ever get rid of that old hammer either.

Back about forty years ago, other folks here in Greenfield Center knew that Jess Bowman was always one for saving things. So, just as a matter of course, they'd let him know when there was something they were getting rid of that he might be able to use. Usually, it was something too big for them to be able to get shut of easy, but they knew Jess Bowman had a wagon and a good team and didn't mind coming just about anywhere to haul away something that still had some use left in it. And that was how Grampa Jesse came by those used shingles.

It seems that Roy Ormsby, up to Lake Desolation, had a camp that he was fixin' up. First thing Roy did was to take off the old wooden shingles. He didn't rip 'em off every which way, like folks do now, but he pulled the nails one by one and laid those shingles out in neat piles on the ground. It took him pretty nigh the whole day and when he was done, he said to one of the Daniels boys—who he knew was heading down to Bowman's Store—"You happen to see anyone who might have some use for these perfectly good used shingles, you just might let 'em know I'm givin' 'em away, first come, first served."

Well, as soon as Grampa Jesse heard about those shingles just waiting up there in neat stacks to be taken away, you know what he decided. Grama Bowman tried to talk him out of it. It was just supper time and even though it was high summer and the days were good and long, there was no way as how he could take his team the ten miles up to Lake Desolation and back before midnight. But Grampa Jesse's mind had been made up quicker than a cat can lick an ear.

"The least you can do," Grama Bowman said, "is wait till after you've had your supper. If you're so hot on climbing Fool's Hill in a hurry, it's still going to be there after you've eaten."

Grampa Jesse had been working all day and he was hungry enough to eat a horse and chase its rider, so he agreed. He sat down, gulped his dinner, and then went out to hitch up the team. When it came to horses, he always had the best. Salvaging things others folks had used was one thing but horses—horses was horses! Some in Greenfield were content to hitch their wagon to a horse old enough to have been in Adam's stable, but not Grampa Jesse. He'd put his old horses out to pasture and let them feed fat on the greenest grass, but those that he hung his whiffletree from was always the best. It was generally agreed that Jess Bowman drove the finest teams in the county, the strongest pullers, the fastest pacers. Some complained that when he was loggin' his team always gave him an unfair advantage. Where other men had to take time to seek out and cut the straight trees to get good saw logs out of them, Grampa Jesse would just down the crooked ones, hitch that team of his onto the tree when it was down and just draw it out straight!

By the time Grampa Jesse got his team hitched and the wagon out of the yard, the sun was about to set. Had it been light, he could have made the run up to the lake in half the time of a man with a normal team, but now that it was getting dark he knew he'd have to take his time. On a summer's night like this folks would be out walking on the Middle Grove Road and if he was to go full speed with that team of his he'd overtake folks and run 'em down before they even knew a team was coming. So, with lanterns burning on each corner of his rig, he set out at a measured pace for Lake Desolation and pulled up to Roy Ormsby's camp just at midnight. And sure enough, just as he'd been told, there were those shingles with a note on them that he figgered read "Help Yourself."

As good luck would have it, there was a full moon that summer night and what with the light from that bright old fella in the night sky and the lanterns on his wagon, Grampa Jesse could make things out just about as good as in the day time. Or at least he would have been able to if he'd been wearing glasses with the right prescription. That was why he figgered that note from Roy Ormsby said "Help Yourself," even though he wasn't exactly able to read it. Grampa Jesse's eyesight was not bad at all except when it come to seeing things close up, so he'd brought some glasses along to help him out some. The glasses he'd brought with him, though, weren't his own. He'd misplaced them but had brought along one of the ten or twelve pairs he'd salvaged from here and there. The ones he had, in fact, were an old pair of bifocals that had been given to him by one of his wife's brothers who'd gotten a new prescription. Grampa Jesse was partial to those glasses because of their real tortoiseshell frames. It was true that when he put them on things got a little wavery—sort of as if he was looking around under water—but it was plain to him that those glasses had plenty of seeing left in them and not using them would have been a waste.

There was no one else around, but that didn't bother Grampa Jesse. After a good meal and a cool night ride he was feeling full of vim and vinegar. He set to picking up those piles of shingles and packing them into the wagon. It was a clear night without a cloud in the sky. By the time he finished packing those wooden shingles in he could feel how much colder it had gotten and he knew that even though it was still summer, there would be a light frost on the ground in the morning, the sort we get up in the mountains as soon as late July some years.

Grampa Jesse pulled his old beach jacket out from under the wagon seat and put it on. Then he looked up at that smiling man up in the moon and grinned back at him, feeling good about the work he'd just done and those perfectly good shingles he'd gotten. And he knew just the place for them, right on the south-eastern wall of the house. All he'd have to do would be to buy some nails. But then, looking around his feet, by the light of that moon and his lanterns he could see the old bent nails that Roy Ormsby had let fall to the ground. Grampa Jesse picked one up. It was brown and not exactly straight, but it still had some use left in it. As a matter of fact, he'd always enjoyed straightening out old nails. He could bend a nail back to true with one pound faster than a man could draw a breath. So he began picking those bent nails up, filling the pockets of his beach jacket with them.

By the time he was done, from the place where the moon hung in the sky he figured it was close to three in the morning. He didn't bother to look at his old pocket watch. Its hands were permanently stuck at 6 o'clock so he knew it wasn't going to be right yet if he looked at it. That watch being stuck at the same time didn't make it any less valuable to him. As he always told me, it was more reliable than most people because you could always count on it to be right twice every day.

His team of horses had gotten a good rest, sleeping where they stood in their traces, and that cool night air was so bracing that he didn't feel a bit weary. He hopped right onto his wagon, snapped the reins, and those horses swung the wagon around and headed on down the mountain at a good steady clip. They got home just before sunrise and, sure enough, just as he had expected the front lawn there on the southeast side of the house was just as white as could be with early summer frost. He still wasn't feel tuckered out, so he decided he'd get right to work. He hopped off the wagon, piled a stack of shingles next to that wall, pulled his old hammer out and reached into his pocket for one of those bent nails he'd saved. That was when he discovered that pocket was one of the ones he'd put his pipe into and burned the bottom so that it finally gave out. All those nails had fallen through. But he was certain sure at least some of those nails had still been in that pocket when he hopped off the wagon, so he slipped on those old bifocals, looked down and, sure enough, there in the frosted grass at his feet he could make out the brown twisty shapes of those old nails. He bent down and gathered up a good double handful and began to straighten them out and pound them right in. He kept on that way, regular as clockwork, till he had shingled about half of the southeast side of the house. It was a lovely morning, just as clear as could be and the sun was coming up and burning off the ground fog.

Grampa Jesse was glad about that fog thinning out as it was.

Ever since what had happened to a relative of his, he had vowed he wouldn't ever work shingling on a foggy day. His Uncle Forrest Bowman, it seems, had a real bad experience shingling a house when there was a heavy fog. Uncle Forrest was up on a ladder working away like a madman, trying to finish before it got too dark. The strange thing was that no matter how hard he worked and how high up he want on that ladder—shingling from the bottom of the house up towards the top, as anyone knows you got to do so as your shingles will overlap—he just couldn't seem to get done. Finally, just about when it was almost too dark to work anymore he ran out of shakes and had to quit for the night. The next morning when he got up, he saw why it had taken him so long and he made that vow to never again shingle in a heavy fog— a vow which was taken to heart by every Bowman from that day on. That fog had been so thick that Uncle Forrest had nailed shingles onto it twelve feet above the top of the roof!

The sun was on his back and just starting to warm up the southeast side of the house when Grampa Jesse figured it as time to go on in and have some breakfast. With the start he'd made, he'd be able to finish off that side of the house before mid-morning. As he was going in, though, he noticed something strange. A whole flock of robins was just sittin' there and starin' up at the side of the house where he'd just nailed on those shingles. No accountin' for how a bird will act, he thought, then he went on in.

Grama Bowman had heard him pounding for the last hour or so and she had known he'd be in before long and gotten his breakfast ready. It was the usual menu—five pounds of bacon, ten gallons of coffee, a gross of pancakes and enough maple syrup to drown a cat in. The Bowmans always liked their maple syrup. It was Uncle Forrest Bowman who had the greatest love for that sweet sap of the woodlands. He would never use a napkin on account of the fact that he had a full face beard and he said that did an adequate job of sopping up whatever didn't make it from his fork to his lips. As a matter of fact, they would shave that beard off of him every spring, boil it down, and get exactly twenty-eight quarts of high-grade maple syrup.

As he sat down for his breakfast, Grampa Jesse was feeling proud as a peacock about what he'd gotten done before even the roosters was up. "Go on out and take a look at that wall, Marion!" he said to his wife. But Grama Bowman wasn't outside for more than a minute before she was back in.

"Well," she said, "those shingles do not look half bad. But when are you going to put them up?"

"Put 'em up?" Grampa Jesse said. "I already done more than half of that side of the house."

"Not that I could see," she said.

Grampa Jesse put down his favorite coffee cup, the cracked one with the chipped handle that he'd glued back in place twice. He walked outside and a whole flock of robins flew up and he came around to the southeast side of the house. There he saw a sight that made him feel so low he would have needed stilts to scratch a snake's back! Those shingles he'd nailed on the house were all on the ground, laying every whichaway. There wasn't but one solitary shingle still stuck to the wall, hanging by a single nail. That was strange enough, but stranger still was the fact that there was a robin flapping around that one shingle. The strangest thing of all, though, was what that solitary nail was doing. It was wiggling and dodging as that robin dove at it. As Grampa Jesse watched in dismay, that last nail wriggled itself free of the shingle, dropped to the ground and crawled into its hole just before the robin could get it. That was when Grampa Jesse realized what had happened. That summer frost the night before had come on so fast it stiffened up the night crawlers on his lawn. With those old glasses of his he hadn't been able to tell the difference! He'd just picked them up and nailed those shingles on with frozen worms.

# GRAMPA JESSE AND THE PATENTED CORN PLANTER

This past April, when I was out fitting the ground to plant, my spading fork struck something that felt like metal. Once I'd dug it up and cleaned it off, I saw it was part of an old patented corn planter. And I knew at once it had to be part of that very one Grampa Jesse bought from the traveling salesman.

Grampa Jesse was always one for buying just about anything sold door to door. He'd been that way ever since the days the salesmen rolled along the log corduroyed road in front of our house on Splinterville Hill (so named for the splinters of wood that iron-shod hooves threw up from the logs laid across to make a road surface) in horse-drawn wagons with pots and pans clanking on the outside and bottles clinking within. As a small child, I was fascinated by the array of patent medicine bottles of every shape and color, all of them empty and lining the shelves of the old three-corner cupboard. As I got older, I was able to read those labels. There were cough syrups, fever reducers, palliatives, stimulants for the heart, the liver, the kidneys, and all the organs above and between. There were "marvellous sanatives guaranteed to be the bane of physicians," emoluments to restore tired blood, and snake-bite remedies. It seemed to my young mind that those bottles had once contained the solutions for every medical

*That corn would come up so fast after you put it in that if you didn't jump aside, those sprouting plants would lift you twelve foot straight up in the air.*

problem short of raising the dead and I even speculated on the existence of some sort of Lazarusian syrup hidden in the dark recesses of that cupboard—perhaps behind the green container that once held intestinal tonic or the blue flask once filled with anti-catarrhal oil.

It was a little later in life that I learned the primary ingredient in every one of those bottles was the same—100 proof alcohol! To realize the full import of that one must be aware of the fact that the majority of Adirondack households consuming such prodigious amounts of health-saving potions were households in which the temperence pledge had been taken. A vow was taken to join in the fight against the ravages of demon rum by refusing to imbibe distilled spirits. As good Methodists, my grandparents stood firm in the Temperence Camp! Neither wine nor beer were to be found within their home. Medicine, of course, was another story. It explained the times I saw Grampa Jesse out bare-headed in the rain, trying to work up a cough authentic enough to jusify a trip to that three-corner cupboard. One time, in fact, he chased a snake a good half mile trying to get its attention when the snakebite remedy was the only full bottle left.

Medicines, of course, were not the only things peddled, especially in the later years when the wagons were replaced by Model A Fords. A new era was ushered in with the automobile, an era of "wondrous scientific advances certain to change the world as we know it." Such amazing advances as sure-fire mouse traps, miracle vacuum cleaners, automatic potato peelers and patented corn planters were just a few of the new gadgets and gizmos loosed upon an unsuspecting world. Much-needed, labor-saving devices, every one.

Now, any fool who's ever farmed it in the Adirondacks knows that anything that can save labor is as welcome as a cold drink of lemonade at the end of a hard row of hoeing. Labor was the one thing our hill farms were never short of in the days when working the land was as tough as bull beef at a penny a pound.

Some of the farms between Greenfield and Corinth, for example, would make a hard man from the flatlands sit down and weep. Those homesteads gave new meaning to the word hilly. It was so hilly at Grampa Jesse's, that it was uphill all the way to the spring behind the barn and uphill all the way back again.

The section we called The Upper Field was so steep that all we could grow in it was potatoes. Grampa Jesse always made it so the rows ran up and down hill. That way, in the fall, all we had to do was dig open the bottom hill and that whole row would roll right out into the basket.

The section we called The Lower Field was a mite steep, too. The only way we could put in the corn was by loading up his shotgun with kernels and shooting them into the hillside. When that corn got tall enough, we'd string ropes between the stalks so we could climb up into the field to hoe it.

Grampa Jesse once tried to use that Lower Field as a cow pasture. It was pretty convenient because all he had to do when he wanted to see if the cows were coming home was look up his chimney. But it turned out that the only way he could keep the cows from falling out of the pasture was by tying them together in pairs, one on each side of the hill. What finally made him give up was that so many of the cows began to suffer from altitude sickness that they weren't giving enough milk for it to be worth the trouble of winching them up into the field each morning.

In addition to being steep, that land was rocky. There's an old saying in the Adirondacks—If you buy the meat, you buy the bones, if you buy the land, you buy the stones. That saying was never truer than at Grampa Jesse's. The only way you could plant radishes was with a pick ax and if you wanted to put in peas you needed to borrow a jack hammer. Rocky as it was, though, that soil was awful fertile, especially in some spots. When you were picking stones you had to be careful where you threw them. If they landed in one of those fertile spots they put down roots and grew up into boulders in no time. When we were planting corn

71

we'd always have to watch it when we got to those fertile spots. That corn would come up so fast after you put it in that if you didn't jump aside, those sprouting plants would lift you twelve foot straight up in the air.

Grampa Jesse used to brag about the size of the potatoes he could grow in that fertile ground. One day, though, Stubby Robinson got tired of hearing him brag.

"All right, Jess," Stubby said, plunking down a brand new five dollar bill, "I'm going to take you up on it. I'll give you this whole five dollars for a bushel of those potatoes if they're as big as you say they are."

Grampa Jesse just looked at that money, sort of sadly, and shook his head. "I'm sorry, Stub," he said, "no matter how much you was to offer I wouldn't cut one of my potatoes in half for no one."

I won't go into how Grampa Jesse used to paint his zucchini squash brown and sell them as saw logs or tell you about how he used to hollow out his gourds, cut doors and windows in them and sell them as summer camps. I'll just get right on with it and tell you about that patented corn planter.

It was a day in early spring when that salesman pulled into the yard in his new Model A, climbed out talking and started to sell Grampa Jesse on the virtues of his new labor-saving de-vice.

"This machine," he said, "is possibly THE greatest technological advance since the invention of the John Deere plow. It will en-able an average man to plant an en-tire field in the time it would take two other men to do a row."

I guess I don't have to tell you that he had Grampa Jesse's attention even before he levered that machine of his out of the back. It was the strangest contraption you could imagine. It had more cogs and gears, more valves and wheels, more levers and pulleys than a merry-go-round. It was shinier than a bluebottle fly. Gramp Jesse was transfixed.

Grama Bowman, though, was the cautious type. She stood

there wiping her hands on her apron and shaking her head. She didn't hold much with these new-fangled gadgets. Even though she was the educated one in the family—having been off to finishing school, she'd seen the elephant—she always held with the tried and true.

"A new broom may sweep clean," she said, "but it takes an old one to find the corners."

Machinery, though, was Grampa Jesse's greatest weakness. The remains of five Model T Fords scattered around the property attested to that. (It also was evidence of the fact that although Grama Bowman's philosophy was "If it ain't broke, don't fix it," Grampa Jesse belonged to the "Just gimme a minute with it and I'll make it run better" school. The long and short of it was that Grampa Jesse bought that patented corn planter.

The next week, when the new leaves were the size of a squirrel's ear, he went out to put in his corn. He gassed that machine up, oiled it, turned the crank a couple of times and it started up. It coughed and wheezed and backfired some, but Grampa Jesse took that as reassurance. That was more or less the way he sounded when he started off each day himself. Before long, that patented corn planter was whizzing along the rows doing its job just as advertised. Grampa Jesse followed behind, pushing the buttons, adjusting the valves, and delighting at the whirr and grind of gears as he watched the kernels of corn zip out of the machine into each neat furrow. He finished that field in record time and when the corn came up he figured he was going to have his best crop ever.

He kept on figuring that right until harvest time. That was when he realized that buying that machine was a mistake. He took a crowbar to that patented corn planter and buried its constituent parts as deep as he could in that corn field. It seems that the ears on that field of corn were the biggest and fattest he'd ever seen. But when he started to husk them, he found each and every one was full of canned corn!

# GRAMPA JESSE
## AND THE
# BULLTROUT

I was clearing away some brush by the side of Bell Brook, the little crick that runs through our property, when I uncovered a small gravestone. I figured it had been hidden there for a good fifty years. For one thing, until around the 50's gravestones in abandoned cemeteries used to have a way of disappearing up in our part of the country, folks being the practical sort. Just down the road from us our neighbors were shocked to find out when they dug up the flagstones in the walkway of the house they'd bought to lay down new ones that those flagstones were all gravemarkers—with the names neatly chiseled off of 'em. One old cemetery up past Glass Factory Mountain beyond Lake Desolation completely disappeared after the Yellow Birch Lumber company came in to log off a section of the mountain where the logging trucks were getting bogged down in places where there were springs under the road. It seems that flat stones were just the ticket to fill in those boggy spots. So, as I leaned over and brushed off the face of that stone I wondered just what I'd read there. The letters were worn almost away, but the name was still clear enough to read. SPECKLY, it said. And I sat back, knowing just whose grave that was. It was Grampa Jesse's pet bulltrout.

*Well, from then on in, that fish and Grampa Jesse were inseparable.*

Now Grampa Jesse was a man who knew how to fish. He didn't do it for sport. Fishing was too important for a man to think of it as anything as frivolous as that. If a man wasn't going out to eat what he was about to catch, then there wasn't any reason on God's green earth why he should be out there on a lake with a pole in his hand—unless he was teaching worms how to swim. On the other hand, though fishing was no laughing matter, there was no reason why a person couldn't have a little fun telling folks about what he caught—or almost caught—after he was done with the serious part.

I recall, for example, how modest Grampa Jesse was about his exploits as a fisherman. When he was asked how big the biggest fish was that he ever caught, he held his hands just a little over a foot and a half apart. That generally satisfied whoever asked him until Grampa Jesse added one minor little by-the-way. "Ah-yup," he'd say, "that's how big we measured it. And around here, you know, we measure them a little different. Not from head to tail, but between the eyes."

The biggest fish, though, was one that got away one day when he and his brother, Jack, were fishing in the Sacandaga Reservoir. They'd just had their lines snapped one after the other, and they was fifty pound test, at that, when Grampa Jesse looked over his side of the boat and shook his head.

"Well," he said, "we didn't bring heavy enough tackle for this one. It's right here under the boat and I can see its right eye looking up at me." And when Jack looked out over the left side and saw its other eye looking up at him, he just had to agree!

Grampa Jesse always said that fish was smarter than people gave them credit. For example, he told of this one trout that lived in a deep culvert just up the road from us a mile in Bell Brook. That fish was too smart to take a hook, but it got itself stranded in that deep hole when there was an unusually dry summer. Grampa Jesse saw it in there, swimming back and forth as if it was studying the situation, and so he sat down to watch and see what that fish would do. There were springs upstream that never ran dry and he knew that if that fish could get up to them it'd be all right. Otherwise, stuck in that hole which was starting to dry up, it'd be done for. He was just considering wading in and tickling that trout out to carry it upstream when that big trout figured out a solution. It turned itself sideways with its head lodged against one side of that little stream and its tail against the other. There was still a trickle of water coming in and that smart trout stayed there just long enough to dam the water upstream till it was a good foot deep. Then, slick as a mink and quick as a whistle, it whipped up the stream before the water level could drop.

That trout was smart, Grampa Jesse said, but it was nothing compared to Speckly. Grampa Jesse was out fishing one night in Braim's Pond, with a lantern and a bucket by his side. He was doing pretty good and had about filled that bucket with bullheads, which was croaking and flopping about in the inch or so of water in that bucket. Bullheads are a tough fish. They'll live out of water for hours if they can stay a little moist and the ones in Braim's Pond were known to be especially tough. In a pouring rain, those Braim's Pond bullheads would sometimes crawl out onto the bank and hunt for nightcrawlers and bugs in the field next to the pond. One summer when the dam went out, those bullheads all crawled two miles overland till they got to Quarry Pond and they stayed there until that dam got fixed and the water level went back up again.

There were trout in Braim's Pond, too, and sometimes— even at night—Grampa Jesse would pull a nice-sized speckled trout out of that water. But what he caught that night really surprised him. It about bent his pole in half and it gave him more fight than any bullhead or trout he'd ever hooked before. When he got it out on the bank, he didn't know what it was. It was about two foot long, had the head and the feelers and the spines of a bullhead, but its body was like a brook trout and it had those pretty colored speckles on it like a trout does. As soon as Grampa

Jesse saw it, he dumped all the other fish out of that big bucket of his, scooped some fresh water, and put that big fish right in there. It didn't thrash around like the other ones did, but just sort of cruised back and forth in that water, coming up to the surface to look at him with one eye ever now and then. Grampa Jesse liked the way it did that and he dangled a worm over its nose. That fish just gently reached up and took that worm out of his hand and then it wagged its tail like a dog, happy as a skunk in a hen-roost. That warmed Grampa Jesse's heart and he knew he just had to take that fish home and show it to Grama Bowman. He filled that pail up so there was plenty of water for the fish to swim around in and then he headed for home. But by the time he got there, the only light in the house was the porch light and so he knew Grama Bowman was asleep. He didn't want to wake her, so he just tippy-toed into the kitchen, set that bucket down in a corner where it'd be safe overnight and went on up to bed. The only thing that he forgot was the cat. They had a big old white-chested tom, not as big as the one Bill Greenfield had way back when, but a grizzled old veteran of many a war. It only had about a quarter inch of ear left on each side of its head and it ruled the neighborhood for a good two miles in every direction. As evidence of that was the fact that virtually every litter of kittens in that part of Greenfield had white-chested kittens in it. That cat had crouched back in the corner, curled up with one eye half open to watch as Grampa Jesse put down that pail which had a very familiar and downright inviting smell about it.

Well, everything was quiet till about midnight and then there was the most goshawful racket you could imagine from the kitchen. Banging and yowling—it woke the house up! Grampa Jesse come running down the stairs, knowing what had happened. He'd forgotten about that danged cat and now it had his fish. He just hoped that he'd be quick enough to rescue it. But when he got to the kitchen and turned on the light, all he saw was that pail tipped over and a big hole in the screen where the cat had gone out. Well, Grampa Jesse was as mad as a nest of hornets with a stick in it. Not only had that dang cat taken his prize fish, it had ruint his screen.

Then he heard the yowling from outside and another noise, a sort of a growling sound. He picked up a lantern, lit it and went out and there he saw a sight he never forgot. That old white-chested tomcat was up in the top of the mountain ash tree next to the house, yowling for help. And down below it, at the base of the tree, was that fish with its mouth full of fur, growling and snapping as it tried to climb up after the cat.

Grampa Jesse ran and got his can of worms and managed to mollify that angry fish by feeding it. After half a dozen worms or so, it started wagging its tail and it rubbed up against his boot. And when he went back in the house, that fish followed him right up stairs and curled up on the rug near the foot of the bed and slept there all that night.

Well, from then on in, that fish and Grampa Jesse were inseparable. When it got real hungry it'd go get the spading fork and then frisk right over to the manure pile and flop up and down till Grampa Jesse dug it some worms. Grampa Jesse named that fish "Speckly" and started to teach it various tricks. Before long it would roll over and play dead—with its little white belly up—and it would shake fins. It was a loyal little sucker, all right. It would fetch him his slippers and his pipe when he sat down in the evening to put his feet up. It tagged along behind him wherever he went, and it just loved to have him scratch it behind the gills—though it wouldn't let anyone else get close to it. If anyone so much as looked like they were about to lay a hand on Grampa Jesse that fish would start growling and whoever it was would back right off! There wasn't no one foolish enough to tangle with a pit bullhead!

There was no doubt but Speckly was smart as a whip and clever as a monkey. No one knows just what that fish might have been capable of learning. The sad fact, though, is that one day as

Grampa Jesse was crossing over the footbridge across Bell Brook with Speckly right at his heels that poor fish slipped and fell into the water and before Grampa Jesse could pull it out, it drowned.

From that day on, Grampa Jesse never went fishing again. And he had that stone carved and erected right there on that spot where I found it so many years later, a testimony to a faithful creature which, had it been another sort of fish, might have been called a one-man cod.

# Grampa Jesse
# and the
# Chickens

**J**ust the other day I was out in the back yard digging a hole to put in a little apple tree. I knew there wasn't much chance it'd be as good a tree as the one that Grampa Jesse had out in the field when I was a kid. That was the one we finally had to cut down because the apples in it were so big that the County Health Department declared them a hazard and condemned the tree for fear some small child might get crushed to death by one of the falling fruits. As I dug, my spade hit a hole, some kind of a burrow, in fact. I knelt down to take a look in it and I was confused for a moment about what it might be until I saw, stuck there in the earth at the bottom of it, a red and white speckled feather. As soon as I saw that I understood. Grampa Jesse's big wind chickens!

Now these days folks are always talking about the wind being strong. I know for a fact that winds do still blow pretty strong hereabouts. Just the other day I saw one particularly stubborn neighbor of mine who was standing out in a windstorm spit out the same chaw of tobacco three times. But from what the old folks tell me, they don't know what a wind really is. Way back when, wind was really wind. When the wind blew folks used to carry anchors around with them just so they wouldn't end up in

*It seems that whenever the wind came up on those hens from the east it blew their feathers off and every time the wind changed to the west it would blow the feathers back on.*

the next county when they tried to walk out to the barn to milk the cows. Folks believed in being prepared and they took certain measures back then to get ready for those big winds. For example, thinking back on apple trees, they would nail the roots of their fruit trees to the ground and glue the green apples on so that they wouldn't lose a season's harvest if a big wind should come up before picking time.

They also had to plan ahead when it came to their animals. When they put the cows out in the hilly pastures where the wind was known to blow particularly strong, they'd fasten a cable around each cow and connect that cable to a winch. That way if the wind picked up that cow and blew it up in the air like a kite they could just reel that cow back in when it was milking time.

And that wind back then was unpredictable! Grampa Jesse told me about one windstorm that was so changeable, it kept coming up first from the east and then swirling back from the west. Now normally, when a strong wind was coming up, Grampa Jesse would go out and shoo his chickens into the coop. He'd made a practice of doing that ever since the day he looked out from the kitchen window and saw one of his favorite laying hens that was caught out in a windstorm lay the same egg four times. He never forgot the look of hopeless frustration on that poor pullet's face!

This one day, though, he got so engrossed in the Farmer's Almanac, that he didn't even notice the wind start to blow. By the time he looked up, it was too late. His poor chickens had got caught out in an Adirondack Southwester-Northeaster. Now those of you from New England have heard of a Northeaster, one of those wet storms that come in off the Atlantic, a real hurricane wind. But not too many have heard of the Southwester-Northeaster which is a storm that is made up of winds from all four directions that come together and just sort of start taking turns with each other. There ain't no way, as my Grampa Jesse said, that a man can make any headway leaning into that sort of a storm.

Well, those winds were so strong that they blew all the feathers off his poor chickens, not once but four times! It seems that whenever the wind came up on those hens from the east it blew their feathers off and every time the wind changed to the west it would blow the feathers back on. As good luck would have it that storm ended with a west wind so Grampa Jesse didn't get left with any naked chickens. That would have been fowl weather, indeed!

But there was no doubt that Grampa Jesse had one flock of confused chickens. He'd started off with two different breeds but after that wind got done swirling around they all ended up part Rhode Island Red and Speckled Leghorn and Plymouth Rock. Not only that, for a week after that storm those chickens went around that barnyard twirling like tops instead of walking.

For a time, that didn't bother Grampa Jesse much. Those chickens were sort of a curiosity and he liked showing them to folks, even after they stopped spinning and started walking and pecking and scratching again like normal hens. He did notice, though, that there was always a bit more dust in the hen yard than there used to be whenever those chickens started flapping their wings. It wasn't until another week later, when he started to notice that some of his chickens were missing that he got worried. Maybe a varmint was making off with some of his special chickens! He took a look in the hen yard and found some holes that were way too big for a mole. Those holes was even bigger than the hole a fox or a weasel might make if they were trying to dig in for a chicken dinner. He filled in the holes, but every day there were new ones and, one by one, more and more of those chickens began to disappear.

Finally, Grampa Jesse decided he just had to keep a watch on that barnyard. He sat there from dawn till it was almost dusk with a shotgun in his lap, just waiting. Finally, just before the sun set, he noticed that some of those chickens were flapping their wings like they were going to fly. But instead of flying, they started to burrow their way right down into ground. As he watched in astonishment, they burrowed right out of sight!

That was when he realized what must have happened. Not only had that wind mixed up all of the birds' feathers, making them part Plymouth Rock and part Leghorn and part Rhode Island Red, it had also blown those feathers back on upside down and backwards. That meant that whenever those birds tried to fly they would go in the opposite direction—digging their way right down into the earth. He ran into that hen yard as fast as he could, but he was too late. The last of his special big wind chickens disappeared from sight under foot and he never saw them again.

# PART THREE

# LIFE IN THE WOODS

# LIFE IN THE LOG CAMPS

**B**ack in the heyday of the Adirondack logging industry, life in the logging camps could get pretty tough. It was not uncommon for a man to go into the woods in the late summer to join a log crew and not come out again until he drove those 13 foot 4 inch long Adirondack logs down the rivers to Glens Falls six months or more later. "The shantyman's life is a wearisome life..." so runs the first line of an old Adirondack ballad. It was up before dawn and out into the woods, come snow or rain or clear weather, to cut and limb and drag and stack—as busy as a fiddler's elbow. It was like that till darkness brought an end to the day—though it was not uncommon for men to work even after dark by the light of torches. As one old logger put it to me, "It was a good 16 hour day, seven days a week at a dollar and a half a day and no overtime."

When they came to the shanty at night, a long building heated with a wood stove, with a bulling area for the men to sit and smoke their pipes and long lines of beds along each wall, some of the men were too tired to do much else but eat whatever was put before them by the Cook—the only woman in camp and usually the wife of the Foreman—and then fall into their bunks. Other men, though, were ready for whatever entertainment

*If you ever chance to stay in an Adirondack cabin back in the woods, I would advise you to shake out your blankets real well and take a close look under your bed before you dowse the glim.*

there was to offer. So it was that swapping tall tales and listening to songs—both old favorites and new ones made up from the events of the camps—was a natural part of the logger's life in the 1800's and the first half of this century. Just how popular a good singer or storyteller was can be judged by the story Lawrence Older told me of how his grandfather Theodorus Older, a new man in town, walked into Crawford's store. Without saying a word, he walked over to the pot-bellied stove and, as he stood there warming himself, began to sing. It wasn't long before most of the people in town found their way into Crawford's. He sang for a good five hours, without ever repeating a song. Then, about 11:00 P.M. he stopped singing, looked around and said, "Any work around here? I'm a chopper." He had a job in short order.

I've spoken before about the animals of the Adirondacks, but there were certain beasts which the lumberjacks in those crowded camps knew better than most. I am referring, of course, to bed bugs and lice. It wasn't that lumberjacks were dirty, it was just that their lives did not lend themselves to modern notions of personal hygeine. The average logger didn't bathe except when he fell by accident into the water on the spring drive. Most men had only one set of longjohns and they tended more towards wearing them out than changing them. As a matter of fact, some men didn't even take off their clothes for months at a time.

Because of the way things were in those camps, the lice and the bed bugs were as common as pig's tracks. So folks just accommodated their life style to them. I heard of one logger who always used to choose a top bunk to sleep in. No one who knew that man's habits ever took the bunk under him because it was his habit to pluck off his lice and heave them down into the bunk underneath him. The solution a good many lumberjacks came to was making one particular louse their special pet. They'd pet that louse and feed it till it was bigger than all the others and it would protect its territory by devouring any other louse that dared to set foot on its logger. Some of those lice got so tough that their owners would make bets on them against another lumberjack's louse. It was a common sight in certain taverns around Saranac and Raquette Lake for one grizzled old lumberjack to butt up against another until they finally decided the only way was to fight it out. Then they would each reach into their shirts and pull out, from its special place next to their breast, their thorough-bred fighting louse. They'd place them on the table and the fight would commence, not to conclude until one louse had beaten and eaten the other and a heart-broken lumberjack had stumbled out into the lonely night without his bosom companion.

Then there were the bedbugs which were, I am told on good authority, ornerier than a crosscut saw and tougher than a halter. Just how tough can be judged by the following story. I won't disclose the true location, since I do not want to discourage folks from visiting one part of the Adirondacks or another. Let me just say that it happened in a log camp somewhere between Old Forge and Blue Mountain Lake.

Now this logging camp was built far back in the woods in a section that hadn't been logged in fifty years. A crew moved in and got a good start on the cutting when, right in the middle of the winter, it was discovered that the logging company which hired the men had gone bankrupt and was not going to meet the payroll. When they heard that, everyone in the camp quit and walked out. Even the cook and the foreman left. They vacated that camp in such a hurry that they didn't even bother to take their bedding with them.

A number of years went by and that camp sat there alone in the deep woods, unvisited by man or boy. Eventually, though, a new company bought up the lease and moved their crew in. When the crew got to the old shanty, it was close to dark and seeing that there were still blankets on the beds, they decided they would just turn on in. They were so tired after that long walk they didn't even bother to shake out the sheets. They dowsed the glim and settled in for sleep. But no more than a few moments had passed before, from one end of the shanty, someone let out this awful shriek, "YOWP!"

They relit the lantern and looked. There, sitting up in bed was one of the lumberjacks. He'd pulled open his longjohns and everyone could see, right across his chest, was a row of scratches like he'd been clawed. They didn't see, though, how any creature they knew could have done that to him and they finally decided, since this particular man had long scraggly nails himself, that he'd just scratched himself in his sleep. So, they dowsed the glim a second time and tried once more to sleep. No more than a minute passed, though, before another yelp came from another part of the room, "YEOW!"

When they lit that lantern a second time they saw a strange sight. In another bunk a lumberjack was looking at his backside and there were the marks there of a set of big teeth which had chomped right into him. Now there was no way, even if he was triple-jointed, for a man to bite himself there. Something strange was going on, for sure. This time, the men decided they were going to find out what was doing this. So, instead of dowsing the glim, they just put a blanket over the light and waited. Sure enough, right away came another yell, "YEEP!" They uncovered that light and saw something scuttling away trying to hide under a bunk. They threw the blanket over it and managed to subdue it, even though it fought like a catamount. But when they looked at it, they were at a loss to figure out what they had. It had big teeth and all kinds of legs, it was covered with fur and had long sharp claws. Finally, they sent it down to the Albany Museum for one of the taxonomists there to decide what sort of critter it was. But those scientists were just about stumped too. It was a beast entirely new to zoological science. Eventually, though, they figured out what had happened. It was this.

It seems that when that camp was abandoned, the crew left so fast that when they left their bedding behind they also left behind their bedbugs. When night came and the men didn't come back, those bedbugs got hungry. They got so hungry after a few nights that they began to roam around the camp, eating flies and spiders and anything else that moved. When they'd cleaned up all the food in the camp, those bedbugs started ranging outdoors. They got bigger and meaner and before long they've moved from catching mice and squirrels to chasing down rabbits. In a few years, those bedbugs were pulling down deer! That was when they ran into some opposition. It seems that the head predators in those woods were the bobcats and the bedbugs were competing with them. The bedbugs and the bobcats started to war with each other and it seemed for a time that they'd wipe each other out. Eventually, though, they came to terms with each other and threw in together. They even started to breed with each other and the result was a hybrid creature, that very beast which the lumberjacks caught in that blanket. It was a bedcat.

Now the bedcat is either extremely rare or totally extinct today. There are several explanations for its disappearance. One is that it was, like the mule which is a cross between a horse and a donkey, unable to reproduce. Another explanation is that it was such a threat to the security of the lumberjacks that they decided to wipe those bedcats out and they hunted them down to the last beast. The number of bedcat heads hanging over the mantles in one little Adirondack town (which shall remain nameless) that was closest to that camp is proof of just how many bedcats they bagged as trophies. Whatever the reason, it appears that the bedcat is pretty much a thing of the past in the Adirondacks—just like those old log camps and the river drives. However, if you ever chance to stay in an Adirondack cabin back in the woods, I would advise you to shake out your blankets real well and take a close look under your bed before you dowse the glim—which is what I am about to do myself right now.

# SIDEHILL WINDERS, HIDE-BEHINDS, SWAMP AUGERS AND OTHER STRANGE ADIRONDACK BEASTS

**M**ost folks who've lived or visited in the Adirondacks know that the area is home to a pretty good variety of large animals. Ask any flatlander what animals you find up in our mountains and almost always they mention the white-tailed deer, the black bear, the red fox and the grey fox. They may even know about the bobcat and the Canada lynx. Some are aware that the coyote, or brush wolf, has made its home in the Adirondacks for the past 40 years or more—moving in from the west to take the place of the vanished timber wolf (which some say may itself have slipped back into the Adirondacks). Some know, too, that the moose have made a come-back, drifting back into this area as the herds in Maine grew larger and young moose feeling the wanderlust established new herds first in New Hampshire and then in Vermont (where one undiscerning young bull moose made national headlines in recent years with its unrequited love for a dairy cow). Today there is actually a small moose herd of more than 20 animals up near Tupper Lake. And there are still rumors, now and then, of sightings of the eastern mountain lion.

However, in addition to those past and present creatures, there are some other lesser-known Adirondack animals which are most often found running wild through the stories of certain folks whose memories or imaginations are a bit stronger than the average amateur zoologist. Let me introduce you to those wonders of nature, the tall tale animals of the Adirondacks.

# HOOP SNAKES
## AND
# OTHERS

Although the Hoop Snake is not a mammal like most of the other animals under discussion here, it is worth mentioning for a number of reasons. For one, it, too, has been relegated in the ecological scheme of things to the niche of myth and legend. For another, its habits are strange enough to earn it a place in this brief bestiary. Further, a knowledge of the habits of the Hoop Snake—which is a truly dangerous animal—may well save the life of some future camper when confronted by this deadly menace.

Perhaps, to put the Hoop Snake in its proper place, it should be discussed in the context of the other dangerous reptiles in the mountains. It is a fact that there are no poisonous snakes in the region of the High Peaks. However, the Eastern Timber Rattlesnake is still found in a few areas, such as the Tongue Mountain Range around Lake George. A rattlesnake will leave you alone unless you step over a log right next to one and startle it and there's no reason to kill a critter which is minding its own business and gentleman enough to warn you whenever you intrude on its territory. Some folks, though, just can't leave well enough alone. One time, as a matter of fact, Lawrence Older told me he came across a den of rattlesnakes up on the mountain above Lake

*It lies in wait near the top of a hill and when it sees some unsuspecting person or animal below it, it quickly grabs its tail in its mouth and launches itself, rolling right straight for its victim just like a giant hoop.*

Desolation. They were just sunning themselves on a ledge right near a grove of little birch saplings. Just to see what they'd do, Lawrence cut one of those saplings and poked it near those snakes. Pretty soon they were all coiled up and striking at that green birch pole. Several of them hit that pole good and filled it right up with venom. Now if you've ever seen an animal bit by a rattlesnake, you know that poison makes them swell right up. Well, before Lawrence knew what was happening, that pole he'd poked the snake with swelled right up in his hand. It got so big he couldn't hold onto it anymore and he had to drop it when it got to be as big as a good size saw log. Those snakes were still just sitting there and Lawrence got an idea. He regretted it later, but it seemed like a good one at the time. He started cutting off those birch saplings and poking them at those poor snakes. He kept it up until those snakes were plumb out of venom and had crawled exhausted back into their rocky den. But by then, he had a stack of birch saplings that had swelled up so good he had a pile of saw logs twenty feet high. He rushed right back down the mountain and got his team of horses and one of his brothers to help him. In just about no time at all they'd dragged all those logs to the mill and had them cut up into boards. There was still a few hours left in the day, so Lawrence and his brother began to build a bunch of little cabins from that wood, figuring they'd make them just big enough to move with a team. Lawrence imagined he was going to make a good amount of money selling those cabins to hunters and campers. They were so light they could easily haul them, but that rattlesnake-swelled wood seemed to be just as sturdy as regular boards, even if it was light as balsa. After they'd finished working, they had just enough wood left over to make something more. That was when Lawrence remembered that his family needed a new chicken house. He got to work and put together a beautiful little chicken house from that wood, carried it home, put it in the back yard, and moved the chickens right into it.

The next morning though, just when the sun came up,

Lawrence heard the most awful screeches and cackling coming from the direction of the hen yard. He jumped out of bed, certain there was a weasel in the chicken coop. But when he came outside, a terrible sight met his eyes. In the cool of the night, the swelling in those birch saplings had started to go down and the warmth of the sun when it rose finished off the process. That hen house had shrunk right back down to the size of a hat box and it had crushed every one of the Older family's chickens. As for the rest of those little cabins he and his brother made, well, Thank God no one had bought and tried to use any of them! Those ready-made cabins had shrunk right down to just about nothing, too. Lawrence was able to make a few dollars off them selling them as bird houses to the tourists, but he said he'd really learned his lesson about swollen expectations and he never bothered a rattlesnake again.

There was a story told once about another dangerous Adirondack reptile. I'm not referring to the eight foot alligator which a bow-hunter shot in Stony Creek one year. Lord knows where that came from! But this other creature was probably an import, just like that alligator. The story goes that an airplane carrying a load of circus animals crashed in the High Peaks near Mount Marcy. All of the animals but one were killed, but that animal was a giant Royal Python. It was early summer when the plane crash took place and that snake found itself a nice warm den to hide in. It was about as long as a tall pine tree and just about as big around, they say, but it got even bigger feeding on rabbits and squirrels and working its way on up to deer and bear, it got bigger still. Hikers started to disappear around the mountains and there were strange stories told about fallen trees that started to move when you sat down on them. Some say that the bones of that snake were found after the first winter, but others say it found a den deep enough to sleep through even the coldest winters and that it is still up there. And it is still hungry. But that's probably just a tale to frighten the flatlanders.

The Hoop Snake is another matter. Hoop Snakes don't grow quite as big as pythons, but like the python they are constrictors. They will wrap themselves around their prey and just keep on squeezing gradually until there's no breath left in the lungs. What makes the Hoop Snake particularly dangerous is the swift method it uses to attack. It lies in wait near the top of a hill and when it sees some unsuspecting person or animal below it, it quickly grabs its tail in its mouth and launches itself, rolling right straight for its victim just like a giant hoop.

If you ever see a big snake in the woods that is grabbing its tail in its mouth, there's only one thing to do. Remember this, for it may save your life. Whatever you do, don't run downhill. Instead, run uphill just as fast as you can. Eventually that Hoop Snake will lose momentum and go rolling back down. When a Hoop Snake sees it can't catch you, it just gives up and crawls back up onto its hilltop to wait for an easier meal. And if you don't believe that's a good way to escape from a Hoop Snake, my Grampa, Jesse Bowman, always kept that method in mind whenever he was in the woods and in all his years no Hoop Snake even got close to him.

# THE HIDE-BEHIND

**H**ave you ever been out in the woods and had the feeling that you saw something out of the corner of your eye? Had the feeling that something was watching you? But then, when you looked, there was nothing there—just maybe the hint of something moving at the very edge of your vision? If that has happened to you, there's a good chance you were being watched by a Hide-Behind.

Because the Hide-Behind is the shyest of all Adirondack beasts, it is impossible to give a good description of one. The problem is that every time you try to get a look at it, the Hide-Behind will hide behind something, a rock, a tree, a bush, whatever is handy. Even the size of the animal is a matter of question. All people know for sure is that the average Hide-Behind is always slightly smaller than whatever object it uses to conceal itself.

When you consider the fact that there are some awfully big bushes, trees, and rocks out there in the woods, it might make you a little nervous. No one has quite established whether the Hide-Behind hides behind things because it is afraid of folks or because it is trying to creep up on them for some purpose of its own. Since no one has ever seen a Hide-Behind and lived to tell

*Over the years, the Hide-Behinds got so good at hiding behind things they started to hide behind themselves.*

about it, you do have to wonder.

In fact, there are two schools of thought on the actual physical appearance of the Hide-Behind. One branch of crypto-zoologists says the Hide-Behind is so all-fired ugly that it doesn't even want its own kind to see it and that they've become so scarce because the only time they can mate is in the darkest of nights when there's no light from moon or stars. Not only that, the baby Hide-Behinds are so unattractive that they are deserted at birth, leaving them so emotionally scarred that they are doomed to a life of painful isolation much like that led by their parents.

The other branch of thought is that the Hide-Behind is actually the most adorable animal in the woods. In fact, they are so cute and cuddly that they don't dare let anyone see them or they would be hugged to death. Staying hidden is simply a survival tactic.

Whatever the case may be, just about everyone agrees that the Hide-Behind—if not extinct already—is certainly an animal which is harder to find every year. The reason for this is simple. Over the years, the Hide-Behinds got so good at hiding behind things they started to hide behind themselves and disappear with a loud POP!

# THE
# SIDE-HILL
# WINDER

**A**daptation to the environment is one of the facts of nature. It has resulted in some amazing things in nature and one of the most dramatic examples is that of the animal which has been variously called the Side-Hill Winder, the Walloper, and the Gouger. Through the wonders of natural selection it has found a way to live on the very steepest of the mountain slopes, grazing on the thin vegetation there and leaning into the hillside to avoid the force of the winter winds. Apparently, over the years this strange breed of creature evolved to the point where the legs on one side of its body are shorter than those on the other side, making it possible to stand upright, even when going along on a hill that slants at a 45 degree angle!

This particular beast, however, has become increasingly rare. There are several reasons for that. One is that over-hunting has taken its toll. Since the animal's legs are shorter on one side, it means that whenever it starts running, it can only keep going in the same direction without being able to turn around. It can't head downslope at too great an angle or, for that matter, go onto the flat lands. All a hunter has to do is start one running and then just wait. Pretty soon that poor defenseless beast will just end up circling the hill and coming right back to where the hunter is

*Apparently, over the years this strange breed of creature evolved to the point where the legs on one side of its body are shorter than those on the other side.*

waiting. For a while the sport of hunting the Side-hill Winder was so popular they even had special guns with curved barrels which were designed to send a bullet right around the hill to hit their target even after it had gone out of sight. I should dispel the old myth that a Side-hill Winder is actually able to change directions by the simple expedient of turning itself inside out. No animal that I know of in nature is able to do that. The closest thing to that I can think of is what happened once to Bill Greenfield when he was hunting up on the mountain on the east branch of the Sacandaga. He came around a corner and found himself confronted on a narrow ledge by an angry bear. That bear charged him with its mouth wide open and there wasn't even time to shoot. Bill did the only thing he could—lunged forward with one arm extended, reaching down that bear's throat till he had it by the tail. Then, with one great yank, he turned that bear inside out! But it's the kind of thing a man would only do if there was no other way to save his life and I know of few other instances of this method of bear-hunting. Bill ran away without seeing what that inside-out bear did next and it's probably just as well, because a bear is a tough critter. When Bill told that story, some didn't want to believe him—until two years later, a hunter shot a 400 pound black bear on that same part of the mountain and when he skinned it out he found there was fur on the inside and fur on the outside.

The other problem which the Side-hill Winder faces which has threatened its survival is due to a tragic accident of evolution. It seems that, for some reason, some Side-hill Winders have their legs shorter on the right (making them clockwise) and others have their legs shorter on the left (making them counter-clockwise). More often than not, the clockwise Side-hill Winders are male and the counter-clockwise ones are females. Thus, when mating season comes, the clockwise males and the counter-clockwise females find themselves at an impasse. All they can do is gaze longingly into each other's eyes. If they attempt to do anything more, they end up rolling to their deaths in the valleys below.

Although the Side-hill Winder is increasingly rare, it is interesting to note that a great many of the cows in the Adirondacks and neighboring Vermont have adapted to that same environment in a similar way. Most of us have seen herds of those cattle gazing on the hillsides and wondered how they could stand upright there, not realizing that they, too, have evolved like the Side-hill Winders into a new breed with legs shorter on one side of their bodies than the other. As a result of this, a good many hill farms either have the milking sheds built right on the hill or have put in the floors at a 45 degree angle so that the farmers can milk their cattle without having the cows fall over on them and crush them. Some of the poorer farmers in Vermont haven't been able to afford the expense of making those steep-pitched floors and have resorted to the expedient of employing cow-stilts which are strapped onto the short legs of each cow as it comes in from the upper pastures. I still recall a storytelling program I did in Niskayuna when I was telling about those cows. A bright and eager third grade girl raised her hand and piped in, "I have been to Vermont and I have seen those cow stilts!"

# THE
# SWAMP
# AUGER

The cedar swamps of the Adirondacks can be a treacherous place. You can be walking along on what seems to be solid ground and then, in one step, go in over your head into a bog-hole. It's particularly dangerous for children to go into those swamps and that may be one of the reasons why Adirondack natives made a point of warning their children about the Swamp Auger.

The Swamp Auger is quite a sight to see. It has a head pretty much like that of a crocodile, only bigger. It has a big mouth and sharp teeth, and it can swallow just about anything whole. It has these bumps on its nose that look sort of like tree roots and when it is in the water—that's about all that sticks up on the critter. Now the rest of the Swamp Auger, with the exception of its big belly, doesn't much match that head. It sort of tapers right down to these little pointy feet and it has real skinny hind legs with knobby knees.

Now auger, as some know, is an old-fashioned name for a drill, and that is just what the Swamp Auger does. It stalks on its hind legs into a bog, wraps those skinny knobby-kneed legs around each other, points those sharp little feet straight down, and then spins around as fast as it can, drilling itself right down

It has a head pretty much like that of a crocodile, only bigger. It has a big mouth and sharp teeth, and it can swallow just about anything whole.

into the mud! When it is deep enough so that nothing sticks out but its nose, it just lies there and waits. As soon as anything that looks halfway edible comes close enough—WHOMP!

Some say, in fact, that if a trail gets used too much—even if it's not in the middle of a swamp, that trail will get soft enough so that a Swamp Auger can move in and then—watch out!

Swamp Augers have been known to eat an entire trail bike or ATV, just to get the rider. It might take them a mite longer to digest everything.

All in all, the Swamp Auger is a good argument for using the services of a well-qualified guide when you're out in the mountains. And if you should ever see your guide take a look at a particularly muddy section of trail ahead and then make a wide detour around it, well, I suggest that you do the same. Especially if you see some bubbles coming up to the surface in that mud hole. There are no records of anyone ever escaping from a Swamp Auger once it has got its jaws clamped shut.

# ABOUT THE AUTHOR

Joe Bruchac is an Adirondack native of Abenaki ancestry. A poet and teacher, he has been writer-in-residence at Columbia University, Hamilton College, and numerous local libraries and Indian reservation schools, as well as teaching Native American literature at the State University of New York at Albany. Featured as a storyteller at festivals in New York, Vermont, Illinois, Missouri, Massachusetts, Nevada, and England, he was brought to Alaska by the Institute of Alaska Native Arts to work with native storytellers from Juneau to Barrow. He is author of seven other books of folk stories including *Iroquois Stories: Heroes and Heroines, Monsters and Magic* and *Return of the Sun: Native American Tales from the Northeast Woodlands.*

# ABOUT THE ILLUSTRATOR

Tom Trujillo is a graphic designer and illustrator. Born, raised and educated in Los Angeles, California, he settled in the Monterey Bay area in 1978 after teaching in Oregon at Mt. Hood Community College. Tom presently lives in La Selva Beach, California with his wife and son.